EXTRAORDINARY
CIRCUMSTANCES

by

JOHN MACDONALD

Published in the United States of America

ISBN 978-1-953904-02-7 (SC)

Macdonald Enterprise
222 West 6th Street
Suite 400, San Pedro, CA 90731
www.stellarliterary.com

Ordering Information and Rights Permission:
Quantity sales. Special discounts might be available on quantity purchases by corporations, associations, and others. For details, contact the publisher at the address above.

For Book Rights Adaptation and other Rights Permission. Call us at toll-free 1-888-945-8513 or send us an email at admin@stellarliterary.com.

DEDICATION

This book is dedicated to my sibling, my little sister Mary Alice, who was always there for me. She passed recently and I miss her so much. So, just sit back, relax and enjoy what I hope you consider a good read. Rest in peace my dear. Love you to pieces.

CONTENTS

CHAPTER 3 Emotional Circumstances

CHAPTER 1

Extraordinary Events

My First Kiss

It happened when I was nine years of age. I was a part of the service community, I was an army brat, and proud of it, even then. My mother, sister, and I traveled across the Atlantic in an ever twisting, rolling, elevator kind of emotion, and what seemed to be, a never ending sea. The trip took thirteen days. It ended with a visit to the English Channel. You could look out one side, and see nothing but ocean, and then look the other way, and what you saw was a troubled, cloudy sky. Everyone on board was sick, and when one individual threw up, it just ran through the entire ship. The really humorous thing is, I didn't want to disembark. All those days standing at the rail, gazing into the depths, watching for signs of life, and there were. We saw dolphins, and whales. No wonder I didn't want this journey to end, but it did. The ship took us to a harbor in France. From there we headed east on a train, another new adventure. When we arrived at Stuttgart, Germany, we found our designated domicile in a barbed wire compound. We service people find a way to meet out fellow students, and of course their parents. It never takes too long, it can't because tomorrow you may be transferred to another city, another country.

On your first school day, you just try to fit in with everybody else, sometimes it works, and others it doesn't. Sometimes you meet the designated bully, and you have to establish your credentials with your fists. At this point in my existence, I was continually at war with someone, resulting in broken glasses, and irritated parents. Then one day, a young lady caught my eye. She was in my class, and so the journey of youth began. We took turns chasing each other all over the playgrounds. Neither of us wanted to catch the other, it was all about the chase. And then the most unimaginable thing happened, I caught her, grabbed her by the arm, and turned her around to face me. With a blushing, smiling face, she reached out to me, and planted a big old kiss right on my lips and ran away. I don't know who was more embarrassed, her, or myself. From that moment on, I think I changed entirely. I no longer felt repulsed by the other sex, no, intrigued would be more applicable. And yes, I became a romantic. Under those kind of circumstances, how could I not?

The years have passed, and many new schools beckoned. On the first day of school, I would look around, anxiously hoping to see that loquacious blonde head of hair walking my way, but it never happened. For years, I would write her name in my new folders, I didn't want to forget, and I never have. I don't remember her name because other events have limited memory, or maybe it's just old age creeping up on me. But, after all is said and done, I will still remember the taste of my first kiss, her smiling lips inviting me on a journey from youth, into puberty. Thank you my dear, wherever you are, and I hope you remember your first kiss. I hope it was mine.

The Hand of God

It is only now the early spring, when flowers bloom, and robins

sing.

Shredded clouds that fill the sky, watch them as they blow on

by.

The growing grass is turning green, up in the trees new leaves

are seen.

A cloudy day, and raindrops fall, the time of year as I recall.

The nights are somewhat shorter now, out in the fields old

farmers plow.

Too soon will come the day for me, when I was born

nostalgically.

I've seen some lands across the sea, a growing time it was for

me.

I've tasted cheese in Switzerland, the snow was cold, and never

planned.

The icy roads where we got stuck, we had to stop a passing

truck.

Despite the fun we all just had, my dad complained, my mom

got mad.

Such treachery the roads concealed, in time our home would be

revealed.

Our trip was on a holiday, we enjoyed it so, but couldn't stay.

And then became the early spring, when roses bloom, and red
birds sing.

Some billowed clouds high in the sky, those colder days are
passing by.

Those summer days will soon appear, the sun gets hot, the skies
are clear.

My days at school will never end, when summers gone, they
start again.

So, this is how my story goes, a year from now, nobody knows.

I'll read some books, and spend my time, another trip would be
just fine.

I think I'll spend some time instead and plant my flowers in
their beds.

It's time to sit and watch them grow, which one is next nobody
knows.

I love to smell my flowers scent, if they weren't here, I would

resent.

The seasons change, the flowers grow, with summer rains, and

winters snow.

We should give thanks, a friendly nod, behold the timely hand

of God.

Wind Chimes

Each day as I awaken, and listen for a sound,

My wind chimes are ablowin' when windy days abound.

The morning's rather chilly, the sun a paler shade,

It's time to get a move on, and some coffee to be made.

I peek out from my window, and watch the birds at play.

They all attack my feeder, I guess they've come to stay.

Those humming birds are stealthy, they like to come and drink,

So rarely do you see them, it makes you stop and think.

Last night they were much fuller, or was it yesterday?

I like to hide and watch them, when nature comes to play.

The days are getting warmer, it's time to go outside,

My flower seeds are growing with a modest sense of pride.

My roses haven't bloomed yet, I guess it's much too soon.

I just can't wait to see them, this May or early June.

I'm not a man of leisure, my patience aren't the same,

A season of indifference, is not a foolish game.

You have to tend your flowers and feed the birds each day.

A chore I wouldn't have it done, any other way.

Changing Leaves

The leaves have turned from green to gold,

The weathers changed from hot to cold.

Some days begin with sunny skies.

And here they change, but who knows why.

The storms build up with thunder clouds,

The howling wind becomes so loud.

The raindrops seem to sting my face,

I need to be somewhere, someplace.

The seasons seem to change at will,

But here I'll stay for now, until,

I hear a languid soothing voice,

It tells me of another choice.

To watch the leaves come falling down,

They tumble to the frozen ground.

At last the snow begins to fall,

It's almost Christmas after all.

Although it never could replace,

The changing leaves from green to gold,

This time of year just can't grow old.

Our Promises

Promises made exclusively, the ones from you and me,

I promise to be by your side for all eternity.

Promises made nostalgically, never seem to last.

Our days together seem to go by so extremely fast.

Promises made will soon be paid for with a golden ring.

My wishes to be here with you, to see what it will bring.

Promises of a trip abroad, a hearty fare thee well.

A trip to Spain, a golden plain, what happens we won't tell.

To sleigh the Alps, and cross the Rhine, a trip down lover's lane,

Together we will see them all, I guess I should explain,

I've seen the world when I was young, those trips across the sea,

I promise we will share our love for all eternity.

A Story Book

To wish, to dream, to fantasize, to feel the warmth from

summer skies.

To search the stars in heavens berth, to travel roads of mother

earth.

To laugh and then to visualize, to see the love in someone's eyes.

There was a man I thought I knew, he looked a lot like me and

you.

His face was torn with tears of rage, a beaten man, now turn the
page.

A story book with bears and owls, a lonely wolf who runs and
howls.

A tragedy from olden days, a fancy car that speeds away.

A walk on down a dusty road, a train that pulls a heavy load.

There was a girl I thought I knew, I fell in love, well wouldn't
you?

Her golden hair and painted lips, I loved to feel her fingertips.

But that was many years ago, why she left I wouldn't know.

Discriminating looks deceive, to try again, a feint reprieve.

Recriminations from afar, a baby step beneath the stars.

Illusively we try to hide, come show the world, a sense of pride.

I need to know which way to turn, 'cause if I don't, my heart will
yearn.

I need to taste your tender lips, come sail away a mighty ship.

I need to know your faith is true, I'll always be in love with you.

Picture Cards

My porch is like a movie screen, where picture cards are always

seen.

As sneaky squirrels traverse the trees, nests are made of grass

and leaves.

Hummingbirds who drink their fill, meet other birds and

always will.

The initial growth of early spring, where flowers grow, a scent

they bring.

The trees are not that earthy brown, and grass will grow across

the ground.

As much as any creature you may see,, the path of life for you

and me.

Each day we walk, a lively step, a search for truth, it must be

kept.

I'd like to think we know the way, to travel on 'til judgement

day.

From mountains high, to deserts low, we'll find the road on

which to go.

A pair of eagles up in the sky, a vampire bat, but not so high.

A cranky jay on feathered wing, a red bird who just loves to

sing.

A puppy dog who smells the wind, a movie show will now begin.

The picture card I have to send, will tempt your eyes until the

end.

Long Distance

There is a girl who resides far away from here.

Why she even calls me up, isn't very clear.

The first time we connected and I heard her friendly laughter,

I knew that we were meant to be for now and ever after.

Some words that I have written, I sent her through the mail.

My heart and soul exhibited, I hope will never fail.

A poets right well proclaimed, I speak of many things.

The voice of kings and destiny and all the love it brings.

If we ever find a way to travel and to meet,

I promise I will bring to you a thought of something sweet.

Loquaciously I dream of you, to touch your lovely face.

You have become my fantasy, the one I can't replace.

In time I know I'll find the way to journey to your town.

Your laughter grows incessantly as long as I'm around.

Keep on living well and someday you will find,

There is a poet, far away, who's always on your mind.

Take Me Home

Take me home, I'm getting tired, and you are much to be

desired. Take me home.

Take me home, and to your bed, until the day when I am dead.

Take me home.

Take me home, don't ever go away, in your arms I'll always stay.

Take me home.

Take me home, you know the place, where I will kiss your lovely

face. Take me home.

Take me home, I hope we make it all the way, close to you I want to stay. Take me home.

Take me home, until the end of time, with you I'm feeling fine. Take me home.

Take me home, let me hold you in my arms, another victim of your charms. Take me home.

Take me home, where we can revel until dawn, until the moment you are gone. Take me home.

Take me home, I'm so afraid, another game that we have played. Take me home.

Take me home, and hold me tight, until the early morning light. Take me home.

Take me home, and tell me what to do, I'll always be in love with you. I think we're home.

Raindrops

Raindrops keep on fallin', agains my windowpane,

Dark clouds are proclaiming, all day will be the same.

All our hopes surround us, just to see another day,

Another storm compels us to stay covered anyway.

Still waters keep on risin', and wash away the ground,

A lightning bold announces, another deadly sound.

Still it makes you wonder, who creates a furious storm,

Who activates and self creates a will to outperform.

The hand of God has spoken, his passion must defy,

A rolling burst of thunder, on which you can rely.

Those raindrops keep on fallin', to grow a fallow field,

He knows how much is needed, a promise now revealed.

Don't fight against a vision, don't swim against the tide,

A promise made, a debt repaid, there's nowhere left to hide.

Those raindrops have stopped fallin' as the sun begins to rise,

Thee testing ground is all around, a gift but no surprise.

Those raindrops are a promise, the tears from up above,

In time we all must realize, He blessed us with His love.

Open Up

Pray to the angels and look to the sky,

You always seemed quite perfect, ony God can say why.

From far away from here, let me make it clear.

We danced until the morning and then sang out of tune,

All alone in the darkness except for the moon.

Don't look away my dear, I promise to be here.

We pursued all the answers and questioned every right,

They only were some stories someone told late at night.

You need to open up to me, I request respectively.

Well beyond all the answers and above all those lies,

I have read all the stories and they offer a surprise.

Look away from me my love, gaze up to the stars above.

All alone with my dreams and my prevailing fantasy,

All my wishes will be answered if you are here with me.

Please don't walk away again and tell me you remember when.

I pray to the heavens that you will whisper out my name,

Tomorrow is so elusive and you are not the one to blame.

You must tell me what to say and don't ever walk away.

I pray every morning to the heavens high above,

I need for you to hold me and express our endless love.

Open up to me my darling and your love will set me free.

Communication

Talk about today, talk about tomorrow,

Talk about a reservoir completely filled with sorrow.

Write about the future, write about the past,

Write about our history where life on earth would last.

Touch my heart politely, grip it with your soul.

Never turn away from love, even when you're old.

Smile at me each morning, kiss my lips goodnight.

Promise you will hold me close and everything's alright.

Wash away the memory, wash away my tears,

Wash away those lonely nights when no one else was here.

Tell me what you're thinking, tell me where you've gone,

Tell me why you left me when everything went wrong.

You know how much I miss you, you know the way I feel,

You know how much I love you, it almost seems surreal.

Until tomorrow takes me, until my life is through,

Until I hold you once again, I'm still in love with you.

Judgement

Been out all night, gotta make things right.

Saw me a sign, did me a line.

Me and my boys, brought all their toys.

Now and then and once again,

Some other guys and all their lies.

We had to fight, went down last night.

No rules were made, I took my blade.

Now and then and once again.

He cut me deep out on the street.

Don't know his name or who to blame.

I almost died, my momma cried.

Now and then and once again.

I ditched the school, don't call me a fool.

It's gettin' late, give me a break.

Did me a line, I'm feelin' fine.

Now and then and once again.

Goin' out again and maybe then,

We'll hafta meet out on the street.

My momma prayed that I had stayed.

Don't ask me why, I had to lie.

Out here I'll stay 'til judgement day.

Sunshine

I've been wakin' to the sunshine and smilin' every day,

My vision of this mornin', well I really couldn't say.

What makes me feel so happy and what opened my eyes?

When teardrops fall from heaven, now that's a big surprise.

The last thing I remember, it was getting kinda late,

The stars were smiling down on me, somehow I could relate.

A rainbow sent from heaven set the evening sky on fire,

My heartbeat kept exploding with a torrid hot desire.

We were walking down the street and I was clinging to your

hand,

I couldn't hardly breath, I had to make another plan.

Forever is giving time, from this moment until then,

My heart is so elated, let's just do it once again.

I've been meaning to be asking you, is this only just a dream?

Together here this morning, I think we're quite a team.

Behold this brilliant morning, and there hardly is a cloud,

When you are standing here beside me, it just makes me sort of

proud.

Our rainbow keeps on shining on a meadow blessed with dew,

A taciturn old message sent, I'm so in love with you.

Winds of Time

Swept away on winds of time, a bus, a train, a car,

It doesn't really feel the same, no matter who you are.

Dignity, apathy, mother nature's lure,

A peaceful search for happiness, where nothing is secure.

Swept away on sheets of rain, when thunder rules the night,

A river flows above its banks, the birds all take to flight.

Tenaciously, determinedly, you try to make it home,

The time it takes to hesitate, you feel so all alone.

Swept away by destiny, a face, a look, a name,

It doesn't matter who you are, or why you would complain.

You need to pause and realize, this is your final test.

Swept away on winds of time, a date with history,

A quite look, the time it took, at last it set you free.

Come Sail With Me

Intrusively delightful, a massive sailing ship,

A river flowing to the sea embarking on a trip.

The sails aloft, a northern wind, a search for infamy,

The clouds parade across the sky, come sail along with me.

Just beyond the harbor roads, our journey has begun,

The captain knows, but seldom shows he's lost without the sun.

His mapped charade the plans were made, to sail before the

dawn.

The friends we met and won't forget, despite the fact they're

gone.

The waves so high, came crashing by and thrash across the

bow,

We dip and yaw from side to side and disappear somehow,

A sailor high up in the shrouds, a glass held to his eye,

A blessed sound is coming down, land ahoy the cry.

Our trip is done, a languid sun upon the far horizon,

Come lend a hand, another man was all just quite surprisin'.

To board the ship, another trip, we all must contemplate,

Come sail with me across the sea, but darlin' don't be late.

Life @ Love

Life and love resiliently, define another stormy day.

The clouds from heaven, a lightening bolt, describe a

judgement from far away.

A touch, a kiss, a distant look, a lost companion from

yesteryear.

The raindrops falling from your eyes, won't hide the pain or

disappear.

A breath of wind, a woman's scent, a touch of class you know so well.

A day remembered from the past, your future journey into hell.

I used to think about tomorrow, I only want what's best for you.

That doesn't mean it hurts me less, you need to tell me what to to.

Life and love will come and go, another storm at last has ended.

Another post card from the past, my love for you is well intended.

A lonely day, a dying sun, the moon above the far horizon,

Another day of history, a word from you would be surprisin'.

I walk along a distant shore, the wind compels a rising tide,

Berift of love or fantasy, I know there is nowhere to hide.

The clouds are gone, the night is warm, I gaze into the stars above,

I think about this girl I knew and of an everlasting love.

Capriciously

Come with me capriciously and search the fields of time.

If ever we were meant to be, you know what's on my mind.

From mountain tops, to fallow fields, or windy days at sea,

I know the look deep in your eyes, come sail away with me.

A darkened road still beckons me to find my way back home.

A crowded bus, a lonely train, at least I'm not alone.

A trip through space, another world and you're not far away.

Each night I hear the bluebird's song, it's time for us to play.

Another man once had a plan, his name I never knew.

A lonely face you must replace, he wasn't right for you.

Come to me capriciously and dance until the dawn.

The music's playing through the night, I hear our favorite song.

Each time I hold you in my arms and whisper in your ear,

You know that I'm in love with you, and always was my dear.

I Reminisce

We were young, our hearts were free, at times like this, I

reminisce.

We traveled far across the land, none of this was really planned,

and still, I reminisce.

My mom and dad sometimes were sad, I think about the fun we

had.

We had a pet, I don't regret, I brushed him until my folks got

mad.

In our car, we went so far, on all of this, I reminisce.

Together we went o'er the sea, a trip to find our destiny.

Forever more, a foreign shore, oh yes, I surely reminisce.

We took a train, it often rained, we traveled to another place.

Another school with different rules and still I seem to reminisce.

A trip back home, we're not alone, another busy port of call.

A homeward state, it sure looked great, and me I always

reminisce.

We drove across the Golden Gate and then on through the

northern states.

The Boston Bruins were hard to beat, we lived upon a busy

street.

New Orleans is a frantic town, where different music can be

found.

In Denver you can see the hills, where skiers go to get their

thrills.

We settled on the mid west plains, where K.C. has a lot of

trains.

A busy life, it seemed alright and most all, I reminisce.

I wrote a book, a different look, I'm hoping you will think of me.

I have a plan, please understand, a different kind of history.

My written word, I think you heard, is all about a lover's glance.

A fateful sound is all around, I had to take another chance.

I wished upon a falling star, it told me what I had to do,

I'll reminisce the whole night through and spend my life in love

with you.

A Certain Someone

I awoke again this morning, I had something on my mind.

A vivid vision from the past, somewhat gracious, always kind.

Like a storybook from heaven, a beaming smile meant just for

me.

I can't wait to read the ending, a vital link with history.

I must be getting older, as the sun begins to fade,

I can't see beyond tomorrow or recall the plans were made.

There used to be a reason to get my body out of bed,

With a final cup of coffee and a story that I read.

My mind just isn't working, is it you or only me?

I remember times together, a gentle smile of dignity.

When we went our separate ways, it didn't last so very long,

Like a little taste of heaven, where we played our favorite song.

When I go to sleep this evening, with a vision on my mind,

I can see a certain someone, or am I simply going blind.

There is something I should tell you, long before you ever go,

From this moment 'til forever, I will always love you so.

Movin' On

I must be movin' on now that you're gone, gone, gone.

Another town, another state, be on your way, don't hesitate.

You're movin' on, away from me, you must have found your

destiny.

Along the shore, a sandy beach, so hard to find or try to reach.

I miss you more and more each day, I don't know how to find

my way.

I must be movin' on now that you're gone, gone, gone.

The seasons change from fall to spring, don't know what next
year will bring.

The raindrops fall a cloudy day, the wintertime just seems to
stay.

I just can't sleep alone at night and yet I'm hoping you're
alright.

The breeze is up, the tide is in, where on earth do I begin?

A shallow sea beyond the shore, I simply miss you more and
more.

Another night, another day, my love for you won't go away.

I must be movin' on now that you're gone, gone, gone.

The wind has died, the fog moves in, I love you so, is that a sin?

Your gentle touch and perfect hair, a love we had beyond
compare.

The winter comes with falling snow, I'm left behind, nowhere to
go.

I tried to read another book, I can't recall how long it took.

My mind is lost, just can't relate, the radio plays a song I hate.

We sang a tune of fond desire, a message from a raging fire.

The night has gone, it turned to grey, I'll love you 'til my

judgement day.

I must be movin' on, now that you're gone, gone, gone.

Where Are You?

I've traveled near and traveled far, had a beer in a local bar,

And then I asked just where you are?

I took a ship across the sea, thought I knew where I should be,

A question popped into my head, am I alive or maybe dead?

I worked a farm outside of town, thought I knew what's going

down,

And still I wonder just where you are?

I knew a gal, gave her a kiss, a subtle touch I wouldn't miss,

She touched my heart, got in my head, we spent the night alone

in bed.

Life's a tragic mystery, above all else I had to see,

You have become a part of me, so where are you?

The road's a lonely part of me, it's where I found my destiny,

And yet I don't know who you are.

A look, a kiss, a guaranty you'll always be a part of me,

A lovely smile, deceptive eyes, a love I never could disguise.

I almost died some time ago and still one thing I need to know,

Where are you?

Until I see the end of time, I have to ask will you be mine?

Until

Until the clouds go passing by,

Until a teardrop fills my eye,

Until we watch a falling star,

Until I know just where you are,

Until my dreams all come to be,

Until you're lying next to me,

Until the night becomes the day,

Until you tell me you will stay,

Until I hold your hand in mine,

Until we see the end of time,

Until we sail across the sea,

Until we find our place to be,

Until tomorrow is today,

And loving you will never go away.

Promises

There you stand, so close to me,

I want you here eternally.

Reluctant rare decisions, an invigorating plan,

It's a glorious new morning, and this is who I am.

We awakened here together, and then you ran away,

With no communication, still I promise I will stay.

Whenever you would want me, just bellow out my name,

With you I'm always smiling, but who would dare complain.

I held you close last night, as we traced the fallow moon,

When you began to wander, not too early, but too soon.

If we were to stay together, who knows where we could go?

It happened much too quickly, and frustrations began to grow.

There you are, here I am, a promise meant to keep,

I'll always be around for you, even in my sleep.

I'll purchase some precious flowers, an Orchid maybe two,

I'll hold you close forever, but only if you want me to.

An insightful odd old memory, with a devious new plan,

I'll pretend you always want me here, forever and rather than,

I watch the stars up in the sky continuing to shine,

If you would only say to me, my darling you are mine.

I need some self assurance, just give me one more chance,

I will always cherish you, and pursue our true romance.

My love is yours forever, you know this is much true,

I promise you a lifetime, to be spent in love with you.

A Seasons Change

The nights are long, and days grow short, as springtime shows

its face.

The trees and leaves are well received, and cannot be replaced.

The seasons change four times a year, the weather does the

same.

From winter snow to summer rain, you simply can't complain.

The distant fields of wheat and corn, are spread out near and

far.

The grapes on vines, for summer wines, a substance for the bar.

A gentle breeze blows through the trees, a lullaby for me.

A rainbow spreads across the sky, it shines eternally.

The spectrum of a midnight sky, when moonlight dominates,

Behold the galaxies from outer space, where stars illuminate.

To sleep evades me once again, and just before the dawn,

A robin's voice, he had no choice, I pray he won't be gone.

The sun above a distant hill, will heal a broken heart.

Another night, a pure delight, as nature dominates.

The seeds that grow, in fields we know, it's time to celebrate.

Something someone said to me, the Lord is near at hand.

The bounty of a harvest day, and now I understand.

Thank you Lord for all you give, for every plant that grows.

The love of life you've given us, and everybody knows.

A touch of rain, from cloudy skies, as nature shows the way.

A golden field, is now revealed, His love is here to stay.

A Breath of Wind

The rushing sounds of shopping feet, imposing words from

those we meet.

A clashing horn, a passing car, the taxi stand is not too far.

A breath of wind, on cloudy days, the rain it seems, is here to

stay.

A rainbow spills across the sky, a silent prayer you can't deny.

The morning sun defines today, I pray it never fades away.

As snowflakes fall and coat the ground, another spring will

soon be found.

The butterfly and honey bee say summer's here, for you and me

another year.

I took a walk, and smelled the air, I was alone, but didn't care.

A chirping sound, the redbird's song, a blessed place where we

belong

A distant sound, a church bell's ring, a holy man with songs to

sing.

A rushing sound blows through the tree, a vision left for you

and me.

High above, the morning star, reminding me of who we are.

I'm just a man, another soul, a gentle word, a heavy toll.

To live and love, and pray to Him, tell me Lord, is this a sin?

My heart says yes, my mind says no, I can't device, or let it go.

A breath of wind, it cools the air, they say that He is everywhere.

A rainbow fills the northern sky, there is no need to wonder
why.

The lord of hosts for you and me, I pray this is my destiny.

Silent Tears

Tears, fears, throughout the years, fortell a broken heart.

Deceptively, incessantly, a love that's torn apart.

Lies, sighs, don't ask me why, I have my heart to you.

A sudden rush, a gentle touch, I thought our love was true.

Silent tears run down my face, and tumble to the ground.

I always will remember you, although you're not around.

Recklessly I gave my all, pretending you were mine.

Another day without you here, the sun no longer shines.

I spend each night lost in my dreams, remembering your touch.

Another dawn, and you are gone, it's you I miss so much.

Tears, fears, another year, be still my broken heart.

Incredibly, inevitably, I don't know where to start.

Lies, sighs, don't make me cry, come back to me again.

Your gentle touch, I need so much, now and maybe then.

A subtle phase, the morning haze, can't hide the way I feel.

Another day, I have to say, I know my love is real.

Silent tears can't wash away, the pain I feel inside.

I'll spend my life remembering, when you were by myside.

Another night of endless dreams, of making move with you.

A fantasy, of you and me, you have to know it's true.

Mysteriously tomorrow is a moment in the sun.

Hypothetically, for you and me, our love has just begun.

Reflections

Somewhere on the ocean edge, underneath its tidal waves,

A written word, we all have heard, a notion of a love to save.

We swim there every day and night, never fear the ebbing tide,

Although it's spoken in our hearts, there is nowhere to run and

hide.

A reflected sunlight sears the eyes, and makes it hard for us to

see,

Another prolific memory, a foretold journey into history.

I think it happened once again, a gentle cleansing of the shore,

To me it's like a trip to heaven, who could ever want for more?

From the twinkling of the morning sun, I see it well beyond the

dawn,

With a subtle touch nostalgically, I wonder where on earth have

you've gone?

From deep beneath the ocean blue, somehow lost in pallid

waves,

A delirious notion comes to mind, there was a love we should

have saved.

We swam there on a summer day, and watched the sunlight

disappear,

I shall remember for all time, when you said you loved me dear.

The reflection of a moonlit night, as we danced across the floor,

My heart will still remind me dear, there is only you I do adore.

Changing

The hotter days of summer, beget an early fall.

Then the icy days of winter, as you wear a warmer shall.

It seems to be routine, as the seasons come and go.

But it never feels the same, when the wind begins to blow.

In the summer it's so easy, as you stroll along the beach.

But mother nature is just waiting, she has something else to

teach.

Now the days are so much shorter, and the snow's above your

knees.

I think I've got a cold, and I'm just about to sneeze.

In the air there's something different, someone's singing Jingle

Bells.

In the morning I'll remember dreams, that no one ever tells.

I'll peak out through the shutters, hoping everything is fine.

All the roads are unencumbered, and that's such a healthy sign.

It won't be long they tell me, 'til the now begins to melt.

I am so tired of shoveling, and that's just the way it felt.

The days are getting warmer, as the leaves begin to grow.

I went walking down the street, seeking faces I should know.

Today it feels like summer, and the pool is crystal clear.

I will meet you with a towel, come and swim with me my dear.

All these changes are surprising, you never know what's on the

way.

We could be sleding, or go swimming on an ever changing day.

Through a Looking Glass

Through a looking glass, what do I see? A lovely face looking back at me.

Through a looking glass, let's talk awhile. She blessed me with her precious smile.

Through a hole in space and time, I only wish that she was mine.

Through a bend in history, come stand by me eternally.

There was a man who looked like me, he took a trip across the

sea.

There was a man nobody knew, a lonely gent who looked like

you.

There was a man who crossed the road, his back was bent, a

heavy load.

There was a man who took a chance, on endless love, a true

romance.

Through a looking glass, what's your name? Talk to me, it's not

a shame,

Through a looking glass, I need to know, don't walk away.

Please don't go.

Through a looking glass, there was a time, I held your hand,

and you were mine.

Through a looking glass historically, I'll love you all eternity.

The Autumn Leaves

The autumn leaves are now descending, the cooler air is

apprehending.

Those summer days that I remember, soon we will feel a cold

December.

Those golden leaves that fill the sky, another season goes

rushing by.

Out in the woods, another tree, will be a fire for you and me.

The window sill is full of ice, I look for you, not once but twice.

Soon we will buy a Christmas tree, and say a prayer nocturnally.

I bought a gift to give to you, this memory will have to do.

Another spring is on the way, still all I see are cloudy days.

The wind still blows, and snowflakes fall, this time of year, the best of all.

Those springtime rains fill up the eaves, and wash away the autumn leaves.

Hot summer days, and cooler nights, means greener trees, but that's alright.

The swimming pools will open soon, which tells me now it's almost June.

The summer fades into the fall, the leaves are doomed as I recall.

The year is quickly passing by, a windy cold October sky.

I'll get a rake for all these leaves, and then we'll climb up

through the trees.

Those barren branches way up high, are just a shadow in the

sky.

Those autumn leaves of red and gold, announce the days are

getting cold.

We used to jump into the leaves, another chilly winter freeze.

If every year I had to choose, I'd pick the fall, I couldn't lose.

The falling leaves, from coast to coast, the time of year I love the

most.

My Place in The Sun

I am not a rock star, not a famous man,

It took so long to find out exactly who I am.

I have traveled many miles, across the deepest sea,

So many different faces, but not exactly me.

When I became a poet, an elusive memory,

It didn't make much sense, just a day in history.

Sometimes when I am lonely, or maybe feeling sad,

A useless interruption, sometimes just makes me mad.

There was a certain someone, we traveled near and far,

We went somewhere to visit, but never in a car.

We traveled down the road, a gorgeous autumn day,

The towns that we were passing, no place for us to stay.

Eventually I woke up, the nurses knew my name,

And then when they released me, nothing was the same.

I took some time for healing, another day's begun,

Those memories will take me to, my place in the sun.

Good Morning

As the shining sun arises, and another day begins,

So indelicately invasive, I can feel the morning winds.

With each day on earth that follows, and those clouds up in the

sky,

We should all remain in bed, and enjoy a peaceful sigh.

Do you recall another morning, when a school bus came for

you,

When your mother made you breakfast, and you knew just

what to do?

When you walked into the hall, where an education could be

found,

All your friends just kept on talking, what a pleasant morning

sound.

With each classroom that you entered, and those questions

seemed to flow,

There would be another teacher, with some answers you should

know.

Now the day is almost over, and the bus had left your school,

There's something you should have learned today, about the

golden rule.

If all of us remembered, the morning suns abrupt display,

The only thing worth waiting for, when we all go out to play.

As a full moon fills the sky, and the darkness filters in,

I will sleep until the morning comes, and another day begins.

Musical Notes

It's written on these pages, some notes composing a song,

The words seem sentimental, but some how they do belong.

If we paused for just a moment, and heard the intensity arise,

The sound will last a moment, until another day arrives.

The drum and keys combine, with each note amazingly clear,

They dance into the moonlight, and then gently touch my ear.

When all these notes are written, and the years go rushing by,

The notes become eternal, and this no one could deny.

If music is nocturnal, and the night is meant to be,

The darkness of the moment, should last eternally.

The vocalized version of music, a song that we can hear,

A voice you must remember, will last throughout the year.

The hunger for excitement, a version of jazz or blues,

The melody holds an answer, but each of us must choose.

It's written on these pages, some notes that make a song,

When all of us go dancing, then nothing could go wrong.

I've never been a singer, but I've played a song or two,

The notes that I remember, where written down for you.

Moonlight

Moonlight and shadows with memories of you,

Another day, fades away, a startling preview.

Twilight 'til sunrise when starlight prevails,

A peaceful sea, our destiny, on which we have sailed.

The desert sun, you can't go on, and you offer a sigh,

Traveling, meandering, under a red velvet sky.

The story is told, and will never grow old, of dancing with you,

A moonlit night, of sensuous delight, will last 'til we're through.

Moonlight and shadows with you in my arms,

A gentle kiss, we dare not miss, a vision of your charms.

From twilight 'til dawn, the story's been told,

The slightest touch, still means so much, and never will grow

old.

Across the sea, come sail with me, you know that it's true,

Forever is another song, about me loving you.

Changes

Don't go changing to try and please me, for me you are my

shining star.

Don't pretend you didn't notice, I couldn't let you get too far.

Just imagine the two of us had never met,

A future sense of real affection, at least it hasn't happened yet.

Don't go changing your looks, your hair, your smiling face.

Don't pretend you didn't feel it, a love you never could replace.

Just imagine a trip we took far across the southern sea,

To hold your hand, and kiss your lips, this has to be our

destiny.

Don't go changing the way you look or feel inside.

The time is now to be together, and there is nowhere left to hide.

Just imagine what the future has in store,

Our love will last beyond tomorrow, you are the one I will adore.

Don't go changing to try and please me, I love you just the way

you are.

I can't pretend I didn't notice, you will always be my shining

star.

Distinction

In a moment of dissention, when you could hardly bear the

sight,

I could hear the indecision, hoping you would be alright.

I have seen your strong convictions, when something got in the

way,

I can't stand to see your teardrops, telling me that I can't stay.

There is only one distinction, was it me, or was it you?

I must hear your final answer, only you can say it's true.

I have never been a liar, although the future is obscure,

And with another night of passion, excitedly we must endure.

In a moment of derision, a funny joke I've heard before,

I still love to hear you laughing, and knowing you're worth

waiting for.

I have answered all your questions, and now it's all left up to

you,

You must tell me what you're thinking, and what I'm supposed

to do.

I have looked into your eyes, and seen affection growing strong,

Until your last decision, I guess I'll just tag along.

I can't stand to see you crying over me, or anything,

In the future we could travel, perhaps the fall, or in the spring.

Knowing we will be together, redundantly, I just don't care.

I would follow you discreetly, not just here, but anywhere.

In a moment of forgiveness, you reached for me and held me

close,

And for me a strong conviction, and at last a final toast,

Here's to love, and here's to passion, may it last forever more,

Here's to me, and here's to you, my lover well worth waiting for.

Lovers Lost

I confess how much I need you, when you're gone I'm simply

lost.

Every day I have this feeling, deep in my heart I know I've cost.

Every minute, every hour, I remember what we had.

When you said goodbye to love, it surely left me feeling sad.

An innocuous decision to go away to somewhere else,

When I'm left here on my own, still wanting you for myself.

The time is right, the music plays a song I do adore,

I promise to be here for you, now and forever more.

This song we sing will always bring a teardrop to my eyes,

An everlasting harmony to hold and sympathize.

A lover lost, a painful cost and yet you're still alive,

An active task, too much to ask, you simply must survive.

The day will come, too soon for some, a destiny revealed,

The love I'll always have for you could never be concealed.

Impatience is a dreadful word, denying how you feel.

I promise to be true to you, I know my love is real.

A lover lost, the knowledge gained, to find the promised land.

Until tomorrow shows me how, please let me hold your hand.

I'm just another foolish man, who opened up his heart,

The only thing I'm praying for is that we never part.

A lover's mate, to contemplate how much you mean to me.

I'll hold you in my arms my dear, for all eternity.

Only For A Moment

Only for a moment, remember when we met?

Only for a moment, a time I won't forget.

Only for a moment, those days I spent with you.

Only for a moment, now tell me what to do,

Another bold perspective, when you walked into my life,

I waited quite impatiently, and I called you once or twice.

I didn't know your face, and just barely knew your name,

I wanted just to meet you, and to show I'm not insane.

Only for a moment, when you walked into the room,

Only for a moment, why you came I must presume,

Only for a moment, when you smiled and looked at me,

Only for a moment, when we found our destiny.

Another place and time, when I saw your smiling face,

You walked into my arms, a time that nothing will replace.

We talked awhile, I held your hand, I don't what was said,

A vision of tomorrow was slowly dancing in my head.

Only for a moment, that evening we first met,

Only for a moment, a time with you I won't forget.

Only for a moment, I must thank the Lord above,

Only for a moment, the day I fell in love.

My Story

The stories go, some years ago, I was lost somewhere and

sleeping.

The nurses say, that night and day, I was alone and somehow

reaching.

You love and breathe quite naturally, it's just the human way.

You toss and turn, and simply yearn, to see another day.

You sleep awhile, there's no denial, you must to just survive.

Your wounded hand, because you can, thank God you're still alive.

The miles you rode, a hidden code, are left somewhere behind.

A shallow sleep, in dreams you seek, a thought deep in your mind.

The stories say, another way, the future calls your name.

A children's book, a funny look, is there for you to claim.

A lover's song, where you belong, a haunting melody.

Her gentle face, you can't replace, a silent history.

Another tale, you must regale, a vision from the past.

A quiet song, where you belong, you're wide awake at last.

You've found a way, with words to say, how you and I exist.

But, everything you think about, my hold a hidden twist.

Life persists inevitably, and well beyond control.

In every single man on earth, there is a living soul.

The children say, come out and play, the days will come and go.

And when they're one, somewhere beyond, we all will miss them

so.

The stories told, as we grow old, another exciting play.

A lover's look, those trips we took, will last 'til judgement day.

The Swallows Song

Into the morning sunlight, a Diva now appears,

Her duties done, beneath the sun, a sum of all those fears.

The coming day, will soon portray, a hidden inner vision,

A silent look, the hand she took, declares a made decision.

So long ago, she swore to him, a love she meant to keep.

But now he's gone, a Swallows song, lost in eternal sleep.

A trip they took, both hand in hand, across a foreign sea,

This memory, shall always be, somewhere eternally.

Into the moonlight shadows, a woman now appears,

Her tearful face, cannot erase, the sum of all her fears.

Alone at night, there came a light, a new voice spoke aloud,

Don't cry my dear, you need not fear, or end up feeling proud.

Each day's a final journey, designed for you and me,

The final cost, will not be lost, you're love will always be.

Emerging from the shadows, a lady now appears,

Another dawn, will soon be gone, don't hide behind those tears.

Her hidden fears, have disappeared, she found another way.

Another man, will hold her hand, all through the coming day.

Love's a rather fragile thing, it's here and then it's gone,

Another night, of pure delight, to hear the Swallows song.

Perception

There's an insidious perception caught up in the human race.

Was it me, maybe you, or just another time and place?

In a moment of forgiveness, He built a paradise for man.

Was it right, maybe wrong, we know He did the best He can.

As intelligence grew stronger, with an interest in war,

We sealed the fate of destiny, meant to last forever more.

As each battle was decided, and countless casualties reside,

He took us to his breast in heaven, some place everyone could hide.

There has always been a reason for each of us to walk in peace.

Even though the path we've chosen, offers pain that won't decease.

There's an insidious perception preached by churches everywhere,

A decided sense of urgency, knowing He will always care.

Was it me, maybe you, or just another time and place?

In a moment left to prayer, He will show us all His dace.

Is it right, or is it wrong to tempt the master from above?

In a moment of forgiveness, He still offers us His love.

Intoxicating

In a moment of delusion, when I thought you called my name,

I can't believe what I am hearing, or am I just insane?

We just had met, I can't forget, somewhere in a foreign land.

The waitress took our order, and at least we had a plan.

The night was spent in letters, written down for us to keep.

The humor of it all is how, we never went to sleep.

I held your hand, and kissed your lips, and never will repent.

My memories of loving you were truly heaven sent.

The days were warm, the nights were cold, and then you turned

away.

The night birds and their lurid song, have now come out to

play.

The morning sun, has now begun, to dry away my tears.

The beauty of another day, is a reluctant sense of fears.

I told you once, and maybe twice, of my intoxicated feelings.

I never thought I'd be the one beset by such revealings.

To hesitate, or denigrate the way you feel inside,

Won't help you when you realize, there is nowhere to hide.

Emotions overcome us all, and now it's time for me.

My love for you will surely last for all eternity.

Only You

Only you could make me feel this way.

I'm begging you, don't ever run away.

Only you could keep my burning love alive.

Without you, I don't know how I would survive.

Only you, and no one else has thrilled me like you do,

If you would go, I'll cry the whole night through.

Do you recall, the moment when we met?

You stole my heart, and I just cannot forget.

Only you will be my shining star.

I'll search all day, no matter where you are.

Only you, are my diamond in the rough,

And I will always need you're warm and gentle touch.

Now is the time for you to take a chance,

We need to share this passionate romance.

Only you, and you alone, could set my heart on fire,

And in your eyes, I've found my true desire.

Only you could teach me wrong from right.

I'll be here for you all through the endless night.

Only you, and you alone, could thrill me like you do,

And from this moment on, I'll be in love with you.

Those Quite Words

As I recall incredibly, it happened quite nostalgically.

I was broken down it seems, devoid of home and quite dreams.

A restless state of mind occurred, I needed help to hear those
words.

It happened on a winters night, I didn't have the means to fight.

The word of God deep in my heart, I had to make another start.

Those quite words He spoke to me, controlled my hidden
destiny.

I've never been a faithful man, but now I have another plan.

A spiritual side of me controls, a part of me that no one knows.

These words I write I can't deny, or even tell the reason why.

So, once again I'm sitting down to try to say something

profound.

The word of God, like nothing else, I had to go and prove

myself.

What else is there for me to say, I just enjoy another day.

He touched my broken heart and soul, I'll cherish Him as life

unfolds.

In My Dreams

You don't have to say you love me, please don't walk away.

Just pretend you want me close, forever and a day.

Pretentiously I listen well, and gaze into your eyes.

Your lovely voice speaks out to me, I hear your tender sighs.

Every time I hold you close, my arms begin to shake.

And if I never took the chance, that would be a huge mistake.

If you were to say you love me, just whisper in my ear.

I would fall into your arms, and let me make it clear,

You and I were meant to be for all the best of times.

You hold my heart and soul in hand, please say you will be

mine.

If thoughts and dreams, and fantasies eventually appeared,

I would tell you truthfully, there's nothing to be feared.

You don't have to say you love me, but help me understand,

Just pretend you want me near, and tell me I'm your man.

Love's emotions drive me crazy, I wander through the night,

And when your laughing eyes appear, they tell me we're alright.

In my dreams I feel your touch, and kiss you tenderly.

Another night of loving you will last eternally.

Forever and a Day

Some things that I see, are never going to be.

Some ladies I have known, were better left alone.

The darker side of town, when no one is around,

It's harder just to live, with nothing left to give.

Just take me to the bar, it can't be very far,

We'll have a drink or two, to see the nighttime through.

This tragedy persists, and I know I won't be missed.

You never asked to stay, not now or any day.

You had to say goodbye, so now just walk on by.

Some faces I have seen, and touched them in between.

Some lovers I have known, have left me all alone.

Some tender lips I've kissed, forever will be missed.

Those stories I have told, eventually grow old.

Some dreams inside of me, somehow will always be.

Some legends I have heard, won't say a single word.

A part of history, denying destiny.

I love to hear your voice, don't leave me any choice.

Just say you love me too, and tell me what to do.

I really want to stay, don't ever walk away.

The truth will set you free, so come and stay with me.

I'll love you anyway, forever and a day.

Music

Something near, an older song I used to hear.

Somewhere close, a delightful sound I love the most.

Silence please, a rift from those piano keys.

Close at hand, I can hear an old time rockin' band.

Come with me, you can't imagine what you'll see.

Take the chance, together we will have ourselves another

chance.

Hold me dear, and I will whisper in your ear.

Summer days, someone's playing on those piano keys.

Hold me close, and sing a song I always loved the most.

Hold me dear, and hum a song we used to hear.

Understand, I love to listen to our favorite band.

Dance with me, the music says that we are meant to be.

Come with me, and I'll love you for eternity.

Lady Mine

My darning, there is something I must tell you, something you should know. You are the world to me. I think of you all day, every day, and dream of you all night long. I remember places we have been, and nights we spent together. I think about being close to you, holding your hand, kissing your lips. I scent the air, and you are there. I gaze into a mirror, and see your face, I can't replace. I stand alone at work, and really do not mind, because I am far away, on a trip to somewhere else with you. Remember riding through the Rockies, all the snow high up on the mountains, and all those lakes so crystal clear and blue, sort of like your eyes? Yes, and I was lost from the very first time I looked into this bottomless, unfiltered version of desire. It only took a moment, a pause in my state of reality, for me to fall in love with you. Somehow over the ensuing years, I never found the way to express myself, to let you know how you have stirred the depths of my emotions, in ways as yet unknown to me. I am not a young man, but the enthusiasm of youth is what I feel whenever I am around you. You have fascinated me from the first time I met you, and fascination is, and should be the beginning of a meaningful relationship, and it was. You and I both know what happened, and my apologies cannot change the past, I wish they could. How does anyone make up for a tragic moment in time, both yours and mine? At some time, words become futile, meaningless, and useless, sort of like me. Anyway, that's the way I feel.

So, what about tomorrow? Will you still be coming around on your friendly visits, pretending not to feel my emotional attachment? Will you ever truly forgive me for my moment of weakness that threatened both our lives? Is it possible for you to feel the way I do? Probably not, wishful thinking, a hope and a prayer. And so begins another phase. I have never been reclusive, or religious, but in my state of loneliness, I wish you well, and nothing but the best, good health, and something, or someone to make your life worthwhile. Family ties dominate, and I was and still am extremely fond of your daughters. The complicated existence of a young woman can be demanding on her, and a loving mother. My question is, who do you turn to, and talk to about a demanding lifestyle, both yours, and theirs? Such a burden would keep me up at night, permitting even less sleep than I get now. Which brings me back to where I began. There will always be room for you in my vacant world, and given the chance to share, emotionally, problematically, or physically, I'll be there, always and forever.

Believe Me

I know you don't believe me when I tell you how I feel,

But, somewhere deep inside of me, I know my love is real.

I still remember how we met, in a work establishment,

From the first time that I saw you, this was heaven sent.

We went to have a drink, a beer or glass of wine,

A touch will last forever, until the end of time.

We talked about each other, it didn't take too long.

A gentle kiss, we dare not miss, is where we both belong.

The minutes turned to hours, and then I took you home.

I couldn't miss your gentle kiss, a heavenly love song.

A passion built inside us, that everyone could see.

Another night, of pure delight, and making love with me.

Nothing lasts forever, or so I have been told.

Our love you see, was meant to be, and never will grow old.

It's been awhile, my gentle child, since I help you in my arms.

Respectively, I'll always be, a victim of your charms.

I know you don't believe me, but you know this much is true,

Until the end of time arrives, I'm still in love with you.

Your Hands

In the hands of an angel is where I want to be,

Never been in such a close proximity.

In the hands of an angel, I can still recall your touch.

You must hear what I am saying, nothing ever meant as much.

In the hands of an angel, I fell in love with you.

Without you I am helpless, and I don't know what to do.

In the hands of an angel, and our passion lasts all night.

We made love into the morning, a predictable insight.

In the hands of an angel, won't you tell me you are mine.

These ill mistaken images, will last the length of time.

In the hands of an angel is where I want to be,

I'll always want you here, and feel you close to me.

Forever is demeaning, and seldom is the same,

Just remember what I'm saying, and no one is to blame.

In the hands of an angel, when I fell in love with you,

Your gentle touch, that means so much, will last the whole night through.

Valentines

Love is an emotion you are meant to keep, quietly hidden, soft and neat.

Sometimes lost, in space and time, a gentle kiss, so hard to find.

I've tried to say just what I feel, but now it feels somewhat surreal.

And when the springtime fills the air, it lifts the heart from all despair.

Then a certain day appears, and all your sadness disappears.

You bow your head, and say a prayer, to Him you know is

always there.

From days of old, a time of grief, A gentle soul who offered

peace.

He spoke of love, and peace on earth, He tried to show what we

are worth.

His gentle words were whisked away, to be reborn on Valentines

day.

So, lift your eyes to high above, and fell the power of his love.

Fill your hearts, and sing His praise, for this is where He always

stays.

A chocolate bar, or piece of pie, there is no need to wonder why.

A perfect day to celebrate, the son of God who won't be late.

We'll read His words, and sing his praise, and say a prayer on

Valentines days.

Andy

Through the void she came to me, a lovely face I couldn't see.

Her voice now sings a song out loud, to hold her hand would make me proud.

She called me up to take a chance, a rather special circumstance.

Each day as I would now awaken, I check to see I'm not mistaken.

A chance to show what I did right, I hope to have her in my

sight.

From the first time when I heard her voice, for me there was no

other choice.

An introduction, should I reply? She touched my heart I can't

deny.

Every day when I'm alone, I long to hear her on my phone.

Andy is the voice I hear, I need to know, but make it clear,

An older voice my words portray, I would love to meet you

anyway.

Perhaps the future holds for me, a lovely living legacy,

A perfect rose, a love proclaimed, a picturesque and perfect

name.

As time goes by and deeds are done, for me dear Andy is the

one.

Lookin' For Love

Been lookin' for love in all the wrong places.

Known me some girls with incredible faces.

Been lookin' for love, just wanderin' around.

Crossed so many hills and she still isn't found.

Been lookin' for love, and it's taken far too long.

Just got into town, where I heard me a song.

Been lookin' for love, I thought she was here.

Now I'm feelin' tired, I've been sheddin' me some tears.

Been lookin' for love, while fightin' such a cold,

Just passin' lonely hours, started thinkin' I'm too old.

Been lookin' for love, please help me my dear Lord,

Just like a new child, sorta cuttin' out the cord.

Been lookin' for love, and I thought this was the place.

I've been lookin' for love, and I will 'til I die,

Just hopin' I will see her, just can't tell her goodbye.

Been lookin' for love, still rememberin' her name,

Don't know why she up and left, can't say who's to blame.

Been lookin' for love up into the clouds above,

Can't make it alone, I'm still needin' all your love.

Been lookin' for love, so caught up in my dream,

I'll be searchin' 'til forever, or so it surely seems.

Dreams and Fantasies

Dreams and fantasies so elusive and surreal,

They incessantly haunt you but say how you feel.

The morning that follows with clouds overhead,

I'd rather be spending my time in your bed.

To hold you and kiss you and be touching your face,

Alone with my memories let nobody replace.

With a vision of you and your glorious smile,

Just tell me you'll stay here if for only a while.

I dreamed that you loved me and whispered my name,

You vanished so quickly, but I can't complain.

I knew from the first that our love wouldn't last,

But that couldn't stop me from making a pass.

My chances to find you were exceedingly small,

But that would not stop me from taking a fall.

That's just how it is and the way that I am,

To hold on to you, I'll do all that I can.

It's just like a novel now revealed in my head,

I'd rather be with you, but I'm left here instead.

My dreams and those fantasies all shriveled and died,

With my memories of you, oh my God how I cried.

When the daylight is gone and the moonlight appears,

I will still be alone and drying those tears.

Another day wasted and my passion still grows,

An apparition of love, but then who really knows?

The Ghosts of Yesterday

It was earlier this morning when I finally lay me down,

As the daylight was approaching and it nary made a sound.

All the ghosts of yesterday huddled well into the night,

On the winds of our tomorrow, there was no one else in sight.

Every memory you would cling to held a story of deceit,

There was only one conclusion and it told of our defeat.

It is written in the pages of an ordinary man,

You must heed the hidden owls 'til you have another plan.

The viscosity of raindrops funnels down the fallow leaves,

In the history of humans, they will do just as they please.

It was earlier this morning and I thought I heard a sound,

I went charging to the window, but there was no one else around.

All the ghosts of my existence were exposed for all to see,

In the daylight of tomorrow, this is just a part of me.

We must heal the seeds of nature, or bear the wrath of all we love,

In the fairly distant future there is the hand of Him above.

I can't hear what you are saying, or feel the passion of desire,

If we don't prepare the future, we will fall into the fire.

It was earlier this morning when I finally climbed the stairs.

Before I lay me down to sleep, I will offer Him my prayers.

A Journey to Love

To truly love is never easy, a journey bound by many a tear.

A vow now taken from the heart, a promise meant to be sincere.

You touch her hand and hold her close, then gaze deep into

those moody eyes,

A subtle smile still beckons you, a love she never could disguise.

Loves journey now has just begun, the miles could never

separate,

A ship, a plane, or just a car, you are miles behind and don't be

late.

A cloudy day, a sunlit sky, the night you danced until the dawn,

A promise of eternal love, alas it all may soon be gone.

A memory of faded dreams, of places far across the sea,

I close my eyes and shout again, my darling come and dance

with me.

All of this and so much more, becomes a story ending with no

fear.

Together we could change the world, my love for you won't

disappear.

To fall in love is never easy, a journey soon taken all by yourself,

Deep in your heart, you're not alone, somewhere there is

somebody else.

A smiling face, a gentle kiss, loves journey has at last begun,

A tiny ring upon her hand, say she will be the only one.

Somewhere

Somewhere someone waits for me, some day we are going to meet.

Somehow I will meet her there walking down a busy street.

Sometimes I think I see her face, shyly looking back at me.

If she gives me the chance, our love will last eternally.

Somewhere, another place and time, I'll rush into her gentle arms.

Somehow I know she wants me too, another victim of her

charms.

Sometimes I dream of holding her, a passion building in her

eyes.

I long to hold her hand in mine, my love for her I can't disguise.

Somewhere beyond a frozen sea, someone still waits for me.

Someday I will meet her there, our love is surely meant to be.

Somehow I will find the way, through endless cloudy stormy

days.

Her love means so much to me in many deep reflexive ways.

Somewhere across the universe, I plan to meet the one I love.

Somehow I know I'll meet her there, I pray to the Lord above.

Sometimes I think I hear her voice, somewhere inside my lonely

room.

Just come and hold me close, no time could ever be too soon.

Somewhere along a rocky road, the street lights are turning

green for me.

Somehow I will find the way and love you for eternity.

Discretion

Gently, discretely a lithesome breeze can stir the early morning

air.

Mildly consuming, it now approaches, the rising sun will soon

be there.

Slowly moving, and non revealing, a probing look from

someone's eyes.

A morning cup discretely taken, an impatient taste you can't

disguise.

A teasing touch, the stirring wind, perhaps another stormy day.

Despite the heat or raindrops falling, a host of birds come out

to play.

A tiny mouse, a larger squirrel, a discretely searching hungry

bear,

Each of them, a gift from God, a vision we are meant to share.

Gently, discretely a snowflake filters slowly from the cloudy sky.

Mother nature signs to us, an early mornings lullaby.

The far horizon, a peaceful dawn, a sign of life across the sea,

A gentle touch, a certain sound, describes what we were meant

to be.

Discretely from the Lord above, His love for us has long been

given,

Just think about a promised love, and keep up with the life

you're livin'.

Discretion is a part of life, and if it's not it should have been.

A fragile sky, the breaking dawn, another day will now begin.

The Morning Sky

Another day of endless gloom. A disheveled crowd goes rushing

by.

From somewhere on the morning train, you see a darkened

cloudy sky.

The voices shouting in the air, a fulfilling day of enterprise.

A book you read again last night, a view from someone else's

eyes.

The candle light, a fireplace, a warm sensation from the past.

A gentle smile upon her face, somehow you knew it wouldn't last.

A clever phrase, a touching glance, a love you lost along the way.

A chilling thought still binds your heart, how could she ever go away?

Remembering the day you met, the sunlight seemed to fill the air.

A tender look, the one you took and suddenly she wasn't there.

A déjà vu repeating theme, keeps happening to me once again.

A quite voice is whispering, my darling I remember when,

The day we met you asked me if I ever went somewhere to dance.

You smiled at me and promised to take a chance on our romance.

Another day of pure delight, the morning crowd goes rushing by.

I'll sing a song of love for you, a precious ringing lullaby.

My song of love, your gentle touch, defines a day in history.

The passion building up inside will never be a mystery.

From somewhere on the morning train, a voice I always long to hear.

Together we will plan the day, we'll always be in love my dear.

CHAPTER 2

Cloudy Days

Time and Circumstance

It happened on the stroke of seven. You walked into my world. I saw your face, our eyes met, and I felt the touch of your hand. You smiled at me, and I was lost, somewhere in between heaven and earth. What do you say when your mouth is suddenly dry, with no moisture to assist in the ability of speech itself? All I could do is smile, and weekly reply, hello. It all happened so quickly, that neither one of us was prepared. We talked, and embraced the moment, hoping it wouldn't be the last, and it wasn't. We seemed to fit together like hands, and gloves. The touch of your hand truly mesmerized me, and our first kiss created a desire I haven't felt in many years. To me, there is nothing like falling in love, and I have. My heartbeat *quickens* every time I hear your voice, and my sense of speech seems to disappear whenever I see your smiling face.

And then a roadblock suddenly appeared, a self defence and self denial established over a period of time, extremely difficult to overcome. What do you say to someone who is reluctant to accept a new and exciting relationship? We are all victims, affected by our past. You live and learn, or simply refuse to accept a future, built on trust and uninhibited affection. Words alone cannot express the way I feel. I realize how difficult it must be for you. But, my darling, you must realize that you are not alone, not anymore. I guess it must be easier for me, since I have been alone so much longer, and yet, your emotions have run wild, just like mine. From the very first time, I knew, I wanted you, not just for a moment, but for the rest of my life, and I still do. So, until the time is right, or your circumstances dictate your availability for a new experience, a new presence, and yes, a new love, I will be waiting patiently for you to come to me.

Searching

I have spent over a dozen years searching for something, or someone to spend my life with. Somewhere along the way, after untold hours looking into my computer screen, I found a means of communicating unknown to me before. My efforts have been prolific, and several attempts in book form have magically appeared. Now it seems that I have found a new source of interest, and the future looks unlimited. I must assure you none of this ever seemed possible, at least not to me. Still, there remains a missing part, someone to share everything with.

Not too long ago I had the great good fortune to meet someone. The mutual attraction was undeniable, and my heartbeat quickened. It only took a look, a smile, for me to recognize the entity I have been searching for. We dined together, and we talked for hours on end. We joined my friends in a public display of a growing friendship. We have even received the blessing of those we have come in contact with, and my heartbeat continues to beat to a tune I am unfamiliar with. Could this be more than passion, maybe even love?

Together we have discussed such a possibility, and I am sold on the reality of an emotional attachment above and beyond my wildest dreams. On the other hand, I have sensed a reluctance, a sense of fear, or denial. How this could be, is not for me to say, but to accept for now. Problematic? Well, of course. The factors to be considered are many, on both sides. The solution, if any? I don't know. How could I? I am just a lonely man, trying to find his way into tomorrow. A certain friendship, more like a companionship, would make things a whole lot easier, at least for me. But here is where the line in the sand has been drawn. I am not looking for a me solution, no, a we solution sounds much better, and that will be my ambition until hell freezes over. I have found my soulmate, someone I want to fall asleep with, and wake up with every day from now on.

Fear of a new and growing attachment makes me smile, a smile of destiny fulfilled, of angst now forgotten, a look into a future unbound by barriers of time or history. These days, when I pear into my computer, I see a certain face, a look, and a smile that tells me, someone awaites, someone wonders, as I do, what tomorrow has to offer. My reply quite simply says, look to the future, well defined by today, my love is yours, and only yours from now until forever.

Talk to Me

Don't talk to me of piety, dignity, or sanctity. Don't talk to me of circumstance, religious ideals, or codes of conduct. Instead, let's discuss passion, sensuality, and emotional attachments, some that touch you deep in your heart and soul, some that drive you forward every day, and every night. Dreams and fantasies rule my world, and they all have you in mind. I can't sleep without your image dominating, intoxicating, and thrilling me beyond compare, 'cause you are there. When you go to church, or simply say a prayer, I'll be there. When you spend your time with friends, I'll be there. When you snuggle in your bed, yawn, and eventually fall asleep, I'll be there. Next Sunday, when you go to pray, take a moment to envision a certain vow, a certain touch, and another version of the hand of fate, it will be mine, off on a journey of discovery.

When I found you, it was a moment of revelation, excitement, and the beginning of a friendship like I have never had, never known before. The hardest thing for me to do is contemplate not having you, not holding you, not loving you. You have become my driving passion, not just today, but every day, every second, every minute I fortuitously draw another breath, and whisper your name. In my dreams, I see your smiling face, gently kiss your cheek, and begin our walk with destiny. Our journey may have a few bumps, a few doors to unlock, and some new memories to create, and acquire. But, to me this is what living is all about. Nothing is easy, it's not supposed to be. So, just talk to me, and help me decide about my future, and yours, because without you there most probably won't be a tomorrow, not for me, so talk to me.

Searching for You

Many a lost soul has gone searching for reality. A moonlit sky, a shallow moon, a lost romance, a starlit June. Compulsive acts, a battle won, for me you are the only one. Hot summer days, the swimming pool, a self reliant kind of fool. A poet's dream beneath the stars, nobody knows just who you are. A candle glows, the wind defies, a hopeless sense of foolish lies. The journey seeks in place and time, a holy vow both yours and mine. The night wind blows, a lonely trail, a lover's kiss will soon prevail. A purple dawn, another day, when all of us are here to stay. A shallow sea, a need to row, will follow us where we would go. I think of us, now and again, I'm not someone who would pretend. The sunlight beams across the sky. A song I learned some time alone I must presume. A fallow field where eagles fly, a trail of tears across the sky. A song I learned some time ago, a sheltered gaze nobody knows. I had a dream, it caused such pain, a trip we took down lover's lane. I kissed your lips, and felt your touch, for me it meant so very much. I'll follow you from now 'til then, I love you so and won't pretend. My lovers kiss, her gentle hand, I try so hard to understand. I knew for now, she had to go, will she return, I do not know. I miss you so, I can't deny, I'll sing for you, a lullaby.

The verse is hot, my voice is cold, I'll sing for you 'til I grow old.

Bookmarks

Touching you, holding you, kissing you, and loving you. These are all bookmarks in our love story. Journeys we have taken over a lifetime are many, you in your world, and me in mine. There are so many places I have been, people I have met, and yes, legends I have heard about. Traveling the world was a part of my education, as it was yours. We often sit, with a glass of wine, and compare. Images of distant lands, well up into my mind, like I just left there. Vivid pictures are painted in the night air, soon to be decimated by the wind. No matter because the scent of you takes its place, wafting on the breeze, blowing through the trees, and filling my heart with passion. This story of ours isn't a new theme, except for us, and I relish every word, reading in between the lines, and adding a new conclusion, one which can only be for you and me. Now, I must place a bookmark in our story of love. You are off on a new adventure, and I am left with my dreams and fantasies about tomorrow, a restless night ensues. I hope that wherever you are, your thoughts and dreams might include me. So, hurry home my love. I will be waiting for you, however long it takes. The night breeze blows, and a silver of a moon, accompanied by the Northern Star are off on the hidden horizon. Somewhere on a distant shore, you can see what I see, and somehow I know you can feel what I do. So, seep thee well tonight, and with another gleaming dawn, hurry home to me, and together we will write the next chapter in our love story. Goodnight my love, until tomorrow.

Inevitable Confusion

Oh my God, in the ever elusive, never ending travails of my humble existence, it would appear that I have quite mistakenly, run into another insurmountable blockade. Just when you think things have turned into a much more favorable direction, everything seems to disintegrate, leaving all your hopes and dreams in a pile of rubble. It has taken me so long to find another person, a girl, who would willingly spend time with me, I had forgotten the feelings, the elation, thriving through every living artery of my heart. How do you adequately thank someone for saving you from a pathetic, nonconsequential means of breathing, and yet, not really living? Mere words, or terminology, cannot suffice. It has been a while since I had something important, meaningful to anticipate, to look forward to. But, it seems to have disappeared, vanished in the blink of an eye. She was here, and now she's gone. I don't know why, or how this happened. The repetitive, deflated sense of a wounded and lost emotional tie, is a feeling I have become familiar with. I have never thought of myself as a loser, but after going through the same tragedy, time after time, one inevitably changes his mind. I have lost someone, much more than a friend, more like a lover, you are meant to spend the rest of your life with, and I would. But, now she's gone. Perhaps I did, or said something wrong, or maybe I just wasn't the man she wanted me to be. Hell hath no fury like that of a woman, and this I mist believe. I could say I'm sorry, but to no avail, as I would be talking to myself, or the blowing, scowling wind. If she could hear me, would she even believe me? Why should she? After all, we have known each other for such a short period of time. They say that time will heal a broken heart, but what about my memories? Some of these are so overpowering that they take my breath away. A certain look, a smiling face, the sound of her voice, followed by a tender touch and kiss, are constantly on my mind. If she was here, I would hold her hand tenderly, and try to explain this feeling, this emotional outburst, and they would all be leading up to those three little words, you know, I love you. And that would be the time and place where I lost her, when she ran away from me. I guess I should have held back, hidden behind a smile, and waited for an inexplicable moment to magically provide the opportunity to profess my inner emotions. But that's not me, not anymore. All my life I found the means to evade any real commitment, foolish and harmful, and not just for me. I have reached the inevitable conclusion, that you are only given a selected number of chances to love and honor the other half of the human experience, and I have found mine. I will be waiting here impatiently, for her return, hopefully she will.

Reflections, Old and New

Reflections, old and new, me and you. Welcome to a world I have come to be familiar with, and know so well. Do you remember when we first met? I do. I was hired into a new job, and after some necessary training, I found myself on line, dealing with an arbitrary public, over products they had purchased. We were on line in close proximity, and it didn't take very much time for us to become acquainted. And in another short period of time, we became more than mere friends. An infatuation? Perhaps. An emotional attachment? Most certainly. A new love? Yes, at least for me. On the other hand, you were dealing with problems you kept to yourself.

With each passing day, and more significant time together, I learned about your past, and the problems inherently difficult, and yet to be resolved. Each of us has a bundle of dirty laundry to carry on our backs, and in our heads. The closer I tried to get, the more you fought to maintain a certain distance, a certain sense of individuality. I believe that somewhere in the depths of your mind, you were determined not to allow another man to ever get that close to you, again. And you didn't. On the surface, for all of our friends to see, we were a couple, and in love with each other. I couldn't keep my hands off of you, and I still can't.

Now, after all these years have come and gone, we are still friends. Even after than infamous motorcycle accident, where I was left in a coma, in a hospital bed, and my source of income was dead and gone, you were always there. No blame was ever offered, and my apologies seemed unimportant, at least to you. It took me quite a while just to recover any sense of rationality, of mental competence. The truth be told, my only true regret, was a temporary loss of temper control. An explanation is redundant. I couldn't understand how or why you allowed me to be around. I essentially had put your life in danger, not on purpose, but still the facts do not lie. These days we see each other about once a week, and find someplace to dine, either at my place, or a local restaurant. Believe it or not, these are the best days of my life.

Now comes a dance with reality, you have gone your separate way, searching for a perfect love. Nothing else would do. And I have found a truly mysterious path of my own, writing. I've been told the written words are a reflection of the living soul, and yes, I believe it. My life has been the proverbial one step forward, and two steps back. But, somewhere along the way, I have finally put two and two together. Life itself is like a mission you have been assigned from birth. A long and tedious journey, over the most difficult roadways, is all you have to look forward to. And, the only thing to medicate, or more easily facilitate, is who you have by your side. When you are angry, I'll be there for you to explore the depths of your anger. When you are sad, I'll be there to wipe away your tears. Why? Because I want to. Every time I see you, is a blessing for me. I dream about being your significant other, but it's just a dream, and you are far away in search of your own fantasy. Wouldn't it be something, to awaken side by side, and realize this is where we are supposed to be. What a dream!

Timeless

Every time I think I know where I am going, I suddenly run into a wall of sheer indifference. Nothing really makes much sense. My world is overcome by a lunar eclipse, my friends have left on their immaculate vacations, and my cell has gone to sleep permanently. I thought my communications skills would lead me out of the darkness, self imposed on my soul, but they haven't. What remains is a storyline, a metaphor, describing the human existence. The funny thing is, we individualistically have no control, and very little influence on virtually anything at all. How many stout young men have traveled to a foreign shore, and not returned? How many? Too many. Service is an ambient proposition, all too often devoid of necessity, and a virtual reality. The very strength of our armed forces is undeniable, but their use for some overseas debate, or conflict, is nothing but a waste, a terrible loss. Once again that horrific wall appears, and renders a peaceful resolution a wish, a dream, a fantasy.

I have been associated with the military for most of my life. I have traveled to foreign lands, and been a part of the strength, the imposing and self reliant force to be nominally imposed by their presence. The terrifying, and possibly destructive part of this scenario is the affects, the memories, these young men bring back with them. To join in search of adventure, only to be confronted by an unexpected reality, can only scar the human nature, and the wounds, themselves can never disappear.

Over a period of time, our men, our soldiers have faced an unseen enemy, one who strikes, wounds and kiss. How does one react? The benefits of an education, the learning process, can offer little comfort, or protection from an IUD, a device for destruction. The wounded may be the subject of a healing process, and a journey back home. But a part of you never leaves the battlefield, never defines a reason for any conflict. And another wall must be breached. A very basic question is, why do men fight? I, myself have never been part of any conflict. Only fools take up arms, rather than discuss indifferences. Only fools look to harm another human being. In the history of humanity, many souls have tried to eliminate a military conflict, and failed.

Hopefully, sometime in the near future, someone will have the way, and means to eliminate any conflict, because the next one, might just be the last.

My Diary

Here it is at 3:45 AM, on Friday, September 15, 2017, and I find myself staring into my computer screen, intently pursuing my thoughts, and putting them down in written text. Is this a form of philosophy? Well, I don't really know. I would assume this title to be resultant of many years of study. I don't think I would qualify. I don't even know what prompted me to begin my journey into poetry. What would be the essence of philosophy? To study the diverse and complicated history of humanity might qualify. A poet might allude to the circumstances of the heart, while philosophy would deal with the mindset. My time for study is a thing of the past, and yet, our history provides the substance of tomorrow, a wish, a dream, a fantasy, and this would describe a poetic intent.

For me, writing is a necessity, a driven force from within, that cannot be denied. Sometimes the words I see come tumbling, voraciously from somewhere deep inside, and then again the current events of my humble existence, are formatted right before my eyes. Incredibly, fore thought is uncommon. I just sit myself down, and let the river flow. Philosophy, or poetry? Well, maybe just a little of both. After a lifetime of arduous labor at a variety of diffuse working attempts, someone has decided to search my soul, and in an unrehearsed method, try to reach out into the human void, and make a difference, to appeal to humanity to pause and think about the repercussions of today's interaction with each other. Better to have loved and lost, rather than to have hidden away, and never been tempted. To whit, I would most certainly agree. I must, for this is a familiar state of mind, heart, and soul. My journeys have been profuse, and at times liberating, and disappointing simultaneously. For most of my life, I have followed my heart, and now remembering is painful, and yet, instructive. If we don't learn from mistakes, or experiences, then all is lost. Hence, I would appeal to every living soul, to live and learn, to enjoy the pause in history that defines your existence, and perhaps to take up the pen of philosophy, to write poetically, about your own experiences, and let the river of knowledge be an unstoppable force for eternity.

Impatience

Impatience is a word that seems to haunt my very soul. When I was young, I couldn't wait to grow up, and follow in my father's footsteps. Eventually I learned about his legacy. It took a long, long time to make peace with who I thought he was, and who he really was. He was just a young man, trying to get along in a world of tragedy, hate, and an unexplained state of illusion. Somewhere, over there, a man who thought he had the right to dictate a future history, where no one could stand in his way without paying an enormous price. Impatiently he tried to dominate the world, and for a while he did. But, impatience has a price of its own, and eventually it presented itself.

Impatience is a world born unto itself. When you think you know what is offered, stop and examine the circumstances. Is this your time, the moment you have been waiting for, or just a pause, a vision of what might be? Just be patient my friend, the world was not completed in a single day, a pause, a lingering date with infamy. Are we all victims, or simply toys to be played with, and suddenly abandoned? Who knows, or really cares? The world today is a conglomerate of institutional disrespect, not of just human rights, but of a need for humanity to stand up, and be counted for who you are, and hope to be.

Every living soul has a purpose, a reason for having been deposited in a world of futuristic demands, a world that maybe destroyed in a heartbeat, an indescribably devastating moment in history. Impatiently a gun is fired. Impatiently a missile is launched, and the bodies do accumulate, and the cities, how they burn. So, where do we go from here? A reaffirmation, a rebuilding must ensue. But, has anything really changed? Is this simply another paragraph in history? Perhaps it is, and I hope it's not. The human brain has unlimited capabilities, and hopefully the domination of others has gone to rest. To live and love irrespectively, without remorse, without defiance, without hate, this is where we are meant to be. Impatiently I await the day when everyone is equal, when we all have a chance to pursue our futures. Impatience is not a virtue, but a vital necessity.

So, wake up world. Tomorrow may be implicitly beautiful, or merely a cloud of contaminated dust, where nothing lives, nothing thrives, and history has been buried where no living creatures will find it. Don't be impatient, we can't or nothing will survive.

Picture Poses

Hello my dear. I have decided to write you a letter, one of disillusion and often, sheer dismay. So, here goes. Tell me dear, where's your heart, your subconscious feelings of passion and desire? I can still remember where and when we met, not the most romantic of places, but neither of us seemed to care. The unmistakable attraction was something I had never encountered before. The physical, and emotional journey before us was both devious and delightful, and the beginning of the best times of my life. Oh, we both carried our own bundle of burdens, which sometimes created a moment of self illusion, but only for a moment, and then we found a means of compassion.

You have always been a woman of distinction, very particular of how you looked, your hair, your dress, your makeup, and I was not, construction doesn't allow for such frivolities. Even then, I thought I cleaned up rather well. Yes, I had a sense of self pride, and I still due. But, the one thing I am most proud of, is having met you, had the opportunity to get to know you, and having fallen in love with you. Some things will unavoidably change, sometimes for the better, and sometimes for something else, but my love for you continues, untarnished, and still growing. Oh I know I'm not nearly the same person I was, but maybe just a little better, more intuitive, more compassionate, at least I hope so, and I really try to be. Just pause a moment and consider, in those years of the past, would I have written down, or even spoken of these truculent emotions running wildly through my head, and yes, my heart.

We both must assume picture poses for our family and friends. But, when it's late at night, and you're lying there all alone, a sudden image magically appears, and once again, dominates the whole of me. Those memories of me and you only lead to one destination, one conclusive pace in time, and you know where I am going. If I had one more chance to change history, both yours and mine, it would be the same, inevitably, because our histories are one and the same. I'll be there, patiently waiting for you, and after all of your preparations are done, you'll be there, pretending not to notice, but you will, and our journey continues until tomorrow, and endless futuristic nights. Sleep thee well my love, and tarry not on reckless dreams, for when thou must awaken, I'll be here forever and a day.

Regrets

Some of these days, I find myself lost in memories of a lifetime of mistakes. Regretfully these may only be pondered from afar. The footsteps of life can be examined, considered, but never forgotten, or retraced. In my seventy years of existence, I have traveled, seen parts of the world most of us will never have the opportunity to visit, and for this, I am truly grateful. You never know what tomorrow may bring, or offer you. Every day you have another chance to impact your world, our world. Somewhere, along the way, I have met my destiny, and didn't even recognize it, or her. Yes, when destiny speaks, or calls your name, you have to pay attention, you have to listen, or she may not speak to you ever again. Believe me when I say this from a position of experience. I have loved and lost more than once, more than I care to admit. Life itself is a glorious gift to be pursued, and enjoyed for the limited space of a lifetime. And what is left? Only memories, both yours, and anyone you come in contact with, is what remains at the end of the day. Your days are numbered, just like mine, and the eternal clock is ticking lou and clear.

So, here we are, you and me, in fear of not accomplishing what we have been put on this earth to do, or at least attempt. None of us is perfect, or without our own delusions of who we are, or what we are doing is correct in our own eyes, or the eyes of God himself. I don't know about you, but I don't want to be forgotten, or remembered as a food, who threw away the most important days of his life. Some of my limited family would regret my passing, while others wouldn't really care, or notice as anything of importance. How sad, to think anyone of us will not re remembered, but only be forgotten like a stirring of the wind.

For me, there will be a written record, nothing outstanding, only a trickle of written attempts, to reach out and touch someone else, to create an image of somewhere else, of someone who might change a life. Oh, I have my friends who I share my ideas, my words with, and when they laugh and smile, then I know I have touched someone in a rather peculiar way. But, that is who I have become, and I like it this way. To reach out and touch someone's heart and soul, signifies that I'm still alive, and impacting those around me. Who could ask for anything more? A memory may fade away in time, but, a written record still remains somewhere on a shelf, perhaps a library, or put away in a drawer, waiting to be rediscovered by a different pair of eyes, a new and brighter mind that chooses to travel on a distant road with me, and maybe then, I will not be forgotten.

Discussions

Hi PJ. We should talk. In our faint, different kind of relationship, we have avoided remembering, and discussing what happened all those years ago. For me, I am simply grateful to have your company, and I think, to a certain extent, you feel a little sorry for me, my condition, and the lifestyle I have been left with. You have found other ways, other men, and your family to keep you occupied. On the other hand, it took this traumatic event to make me realize how much you mean to me. All those days and nights were the best times of my entire life. But, even then we were both reluctant to give our hearts away. To many emotional barriers from other relationships stood in the way. After the accident, which shamefully endangered your life, the aftershock took awhile to set in, to become crystal clear, and for you to turn away from me. I deserve it, no doubt. In retrospect, I lost the love of my life, and you began the search for someone else. Gratefully, you are still a part of my life. I let your dog out to do her thing, and we have dinner together just about once a week. The rest of my time is spent thinking about you, and all the things we did. But most of all, I miss you more than I can say.

I have tried to move on, and as you know, I have found my way of expression. There is a plethora of things to write about, the weather, trips around the world, lovers found and lost, and they all revolve around you. Oh, I have tried to find someone else, someone to replace you, but that simply will not happen. There remains but a figment of who I was, who I wanted to be, and they all include having you by my side, not as just a friend, but as the love of my life. Every piece I write, every dream I have, are all about you.

I don't want to sound redundant, but there it is, I know it, and you know it too. Current events may change my life. You never know. And should things turn around for me, they couldn't mean as much if you are not there to share, and enjoy with me. I have no illusions of being a wealthy man, because all the riches in the world will have no meaning without you.

Maybe we should have had this discussion some time ago, but I didn't want to take the chance of losing you. Nothing has changed in that respect. Yes, I seemed to have found my voice in written form if nothing else. But, after all is said and done, you are still the mainframe of my life, the very fiber of my existence, the reason I get up every day, go to work, and breathlessly await your next visit. I miss you every day, and even more, every night.

Well, it's getting late, as usual, and although I'm not very tired, I guess I'll go to bed, and try to dream of you. My life is more fantasy, than reality, well, so be it. Good night my love, I'll see you in my dreams

A Road Trip

Don't ask me why, but I decided to take a trip, nowhere special, and for no particular reason. I had the time, and needed a change of routine and location. I had a motorcycle accident in 2002, which left me with certain disabilities, my right side, and my sense of balance. It took me quite awhile to get used to a different lifestyle, and just learning to walk again. Seated I am just fine, so driving is not problematic for me. Anyway, I was on the road, and actually enjoying that sense of freedom. I drove into the early afternoon, on a less traveled hiway, and found what I was looking for, a little side road town of three hundred souls, where no one knew my name. I found the local hotel and restaurant, and got me a room for the night. This was a pleasant town, with friendly folks, and I decided to take a walk, And see the town. Walking is my speed, and running a distinctive luxury

I could no longer indulge in. But, it was a warm day, and a peaceful vantage point on a nearby hill beckoned. I started walking with a destination in mind, and then got into a jog, actually running faster and faster, breathing harder with every pace. Oh my God, look at me, I'm running again. I reached the top of the hill, and paused to enjoy the sight, al smiles, and extremely pleased with myself. This had to be a miracle, it was like I shed some twenty years in a heartbeat. I couldn't wait to call my sister with the news. So, I started down the hill, running as fast as I could, reached the bottom in a matter of seconds, and fell face first into a patch of flowers. I laid there for a moment, enjoying the fragrance of mother natures beauty, and then I woke up. It was all a dream, one I've had before. Nothing had changed. I was still an older man, with my disabilities.

It had taken me a long time to come to grips with my situation, but a man can dream, can't he? I walked back to the inn, went inside for a dinner, not too bad, and headed for my room. By now darkness had descended, and I headed back to my hilltop. I took a seat in the gently blowing summer grass, and realized just how fortunate I was just to be here, breathing in this fresh air, with another morning waiting for me to see. Some time ago, I began my writing career, after the wreck, and thought this is what I'm supposed to do with my life, successful, or not. After one has survived, and endured such a traumatic change in life, you look at things, everything differently, and in that one moment, sheathed in darkness, it came to me why I was here, still alive. There was something I had never done, a debt I had never paid, and it was to simply recognize the hand of God, and offer Him my thanks for living, for writing, and for the peace that filled me in this time and place. Thank you God.

Forever to Never

Forever to never would define my history with you. I think I fell in love with you from the very first moment we met, and yet? We took the first steps quite easily, the touching, the loving, the passion was there, to share. We walked together, talked together, although that was your domaine, the talking, insane. Physically we were there, somewhere, anywhere at all, as I recall. The days never seemed to pass quickly enough, so we could be together again, remember when? I do, words you may never say again. Wishfully I would, if I could.

Another day, is underway. Another dawn, and you are gone. The minutes become hours, and I am left with my memories, my fantasies, and they still remain, a sense of pain. What am I supposed to do without you? Like a lost and lonely child, left on the doorsteps of humanity, I hesitate, and wonder. If God in person, is looking down on me, He would hear my cries of destitution, and feel the teardrops as they meander down my face. Distastefully they remind me of better days, revolving rights when we held each other tight seemingly forever, and never expecting things to change, rather strange. But, they did, they have, and there is nothing I can do about it, is there? I don't know. How could I, when I don't really know what happened. Do you?

Anyway, it's here I'll stay, and hopefully you will find your way back home, where you belong, and we will have another dance, another chance to make each other whole again, happy again, in love again, remember when?

The Sands of Time

I stroll across the sands of time, berift of purpose or meaning. An irrevocable sadness follows me, taunts me, defies me. Who am I to dispute or challenge my date with destiny? I cannot, I dare not, for to due so would force a decision, an awkward realization of who I am, and what I'm attempting to due with my life. There were other days, more peaceful times when I thought I grasped all the answers and held them firmly in my hands. In that briefest moment of existence, I was content. I went to work, and paid my bills, simple and effective. But then, everything changed in a fleeting instant. Time stood still and watched me plummet into the depths of disillusion and agony. Was this the hand of God which smote me fiercely to the ground, never to arise quite the same? To this very day, I must confess the answer to this riddle escapes me. My intuition tells me otherwise, but my stubbornness avoids the inevitable. At some place and time I must come to face reality, my reality. My life continues through the hands of fate, or the heavenly Father, someone I have never known, and never met. What due you say to an entity unbeknownst to you throughout your life? A thank you would hardly suffice, perhaps a prayer would be amenable. My eyes look forward, and see a divergent finish, a conclusion of fate and destiny.

I have tried so many times to unlock my heart and accept Him. Mine is not an implacable soul, not beset by ignorance, or stupidity, and experience alone would dictate a final resolution of all my questions. And yet, there lingers, as the clouds of reality drift by my windows, and conceal the inevitable truth. I remain a lost and lonely soul, on a journey to I know not where, and what awaits beyond tomorrow. Fear or angst do not bother me, and I travel on in search of meaning and purpose, for without these vital visions, I dare not gaze into the future. My dreams and fantasies lead me on into the whirlwinds of tomorrow, where linguistically I challenge all who would venture there, including myself. And, therein lies the truest challenge. To realize who I am, and offer to assist anyone who would listen, anyone facing a similar destiny. We who are but mortals, often inept at discloser, or affection, adrift in the sea of humanity, and crossing the sands of time.

Despair

Despair can run so rampant, through a troubled, aching heart. Irrevocably we look upon current events, wondering exactly what went wrong. A broken engagement where families, and individuals are supposed to come together, can illustrate a broken foundation, where nothing of substance has a chance to grow, and proliferate. Disparagingly we try to understand, and seldom do. The worst part is, anyone in such a set of circumstances knows what to do, or who to turn to for answers.

I have spent a forth of my time on earth fighting against these feelings of incompetence, and futility. If someone would take the time to explain what happened, and what I am supposed to do now, it would be especially helpful. No one likes existing under a darkened blanket of reality, or at least not me. I went from an acceptable future, into one unknown by me.

When the simplistic tasks of walking and talking are intensive barriers to assault and overcome, you are left with a reprehensible feeling of despair.

Having been there, and fought against a plethora of emotions, and physical problems, I didn't know what to do. But, somehow, something turned my head around, and provided a different outlook on life itself. I have found my way back through the intrinsic use of words, phrases, and stories. Some of them are escapist in nature, and some a different face of reality. We all have memories, fantasies of yesterday, which are meant to create an improved tomorrow. You live and grow, or give up on everything, and pass away. Me? I refuse to surrender to oblivion. There is so much more to see and do. There are no limits, no unscalable boundaries to overcome. If you are like me, our futures are limitless, and meant to be conquered. I never said I couldn't, and I never will.

Here It Is

Well, here it is, or maybe I should ask, just what happened? Standing here, examining a seventy year period of insignificant, and really unaccomplished style of existing, I wonder, what happened, and who am I supposed to be? Maybe it seems insignificant to you, but when you and your life is the subject, and question of the presence, things become more difficult to describe, or explain. I, most certainly am no one special, not an overpowering individual. I have never thought of myself as a cunning, or deceitful person, but more of a realistic sort of guy. My expectations never went past today, or a scheduled tomorrow, dependable, reliable, and usually right on time. And there it is, time, an inscrutable and indescribable essence of humanity. Most of us, admit it or not, have an essential idea of who we are, and where we fit in the universe that surround us.

So,, just imagine you have been lost, asleep, while the world around you continued in its everchanging, and ever confusing journey into the future, a place that you are not supposed to see, or experience. You passed away on a lonely road, over a lengthy hill, and crashed against a living tree, that epitomizes an end, and a new beginning. I wasn't supposed to see another day or experience the ebb and flow of the living soul. My time was up. My chances were taken, and disavowed.

Well, not so fast. I have never, ever, given up so easily. I have never thrown my hands up, and declared, I surrender, I give up, I missed my chances. No, lost in my comma, but still alive, if you listened, you would have heard my request for just one more chance, one more opportunity to success, to find my way, and I just might have found it. What do you do with your living experiences? File them away as inessential, unimportant, or irrelevant? Not me! Somewhere in the depths of disillusionment, and recovery, I found my voice, my reason for living. My written words are meant to convey an understanding, a sense of peace in the unending search for the bare essentials of living, and loving every day and night. The most incredible, and demanding things and events are waiting for each of us. The question is, here it is, so what are you going to do with it?

CHAPTER 3

Emotional Circumstances

Nature's High

A breeze is flowing through the trees. A gentle stirring of those leaves.

A red bird sings its vibrant song, and robins try to sing along.

A turtle dove coos to its mate, come to me, don't hesitate.

The blue jay often steals its nest, while victims soar and they protest.

As nighttime comes and darkness too, creatures hide, why wouldn't you?

A throaty owl up in a tree, is somewhere that nobody sees.

Suddenly the moon appears, enlightened now, we have no fears.

The cicadas chirping scratchy sound, belies some place he can't

be found.

A stealthy feline in search of food, a purring sound, another

mood. A barking dog somewhere outside, his rattled chain, he

just can't hide.

And when your headlights pierce the night, a raccoon's eyes, a

fearful sigh.

Your garbage cans are never safe, when birds and bugs will

have a taste.

The moon is gone, and dawn is near, another sound that I can

hear.

A crowd of honkers passing by, the sound of mother nature's

high.

The Open Road

I have always embraced the open road, as a military dependent, you have no choice, I still remember traveling from town to town, from state to state, and different countries around the world. So many miles spent in the back of our station wagen, and eagerly waiting for the next stop, the next meal, became a part of every day life. I didn't mind, my mother did, because she did most of the driving. My dad was usually already on station, and hopefully finding our next home. Down the road we went, with our belongings, at least some of them, and of course, our most recent dog companion. I recall brushing him, and sending his hair flying front to back, inhibiting everyones breathing without swallowing and coughing up the residue. Every place we went, the process repeated itself. You moved in and went to your new school. You met your new neighbors and tried to get along, make new friends, and so on again. Racially, I was not aware. We are all just one happy family, a product of the hand of God, with certain differences, but naturally, a gift to be exploited and explored. If we were all the same, what would there be to talk about, what on earth would we question, or have to learn about, a redundant and boring day to day existence.

I would rather wake up today, anticipating a new tomorrow, and any new experiences waiting for you and me. Perhaps our meeting has been predetermined, and all we have to do is wait for it to happen. I'm sitting here, almost beside myself with excitement, anticipating all the new friends I will have to treasure, and to take with me wherever I may go, a picture postcard, a vivid memory that will last as long as I do. Who knows, maybe it will survive, and I can show it off to my plethora of new friends, around the world, and up to heavens gates. I'll be waiting there. Let me introduce you.

Half Empty or Half Full

I have been sitting out on my patio, and visualizing the growing flowers all around me. At this time, they are showing early growth, and mainly green shoots bursting from the soil. My morning glories are reaching through the air, and my hopes for a return of those yellow roses are extensive. Then, my eyes turned to the sky, peaceful now with gentle breeze barely stirring the leaves on nearby trees. A pallid quarter moon, neither half empty, or half full, shows itself gliding through the northern sky. Then, my mind begins to wander. Can you imagine the changes the moon has witnessed on our planet, here in the Milky Way? The centuries of conflagration, of disease, of starvation, and death, earmarking the evolution of man, and yet somehow we are still here, still surviving. Suddenly a mighty blast with sheering flames announce the latest space probe, launched from a NASA venue. The noise splits the air, and in a heartbeat this ship is out of sight. Manned, or unmanned, the television will let us know. Where it is headed, the director will tell us. Not too long ago, such an adventure was the stuff of dreams, at least for most of us. The idea of drifting through spade, where time slows, and the thrill of progression grows nonstop.

The thrill of hurtling through space and time can only be felt by a few, and they can rarely be heard in discussing the sensation. We all assume space travel is inevitable, and the stars are ours to investigate, and perhaps to inhabit. The question is, how would you feel about existing in a space suit, or an artificially induced air lock, pressurized, sanitized, and without the oxygen we need to breath, to live? I don't think I could stand it. I need to smell my flowers and watch them grow. I need to be able to reach out and touch someone, to feel their touch, to hear their voices, to witness their successes and failures. To me, this is the reality of living and dying, not by yourself, locked up in a ship destined for another star, another planet, but sharing the experiences of our little bit of space and time, here on mother earth. I would rather wake up to a brilliant shining morning sun, to feel its warmth, or to see the raindrops pummeling the ground. You can have your journeys to outer space. We will still be here, dealing with the obstacles of nature, and with each other. Why not? Somewhere out there in the early morning hours, someone else is watching and wondering what tomorrow will have to offer Who knows? Maybe we will meet, share a cup of coffee, and maybe something extra, something well beyond imagination.

The Old House

My story begins when I was but a lad of eight years old. My family was a band of scurrilous road warriors, constantly on the move. My father was continuously in search of a satisfying job. It seemed that the maintenance fees of maintaining a singular occupation for any length of time, would simply not suffice. Therefor our old jalopy could be heard and seen in search of a new domicile on a continually, and reliable period of time. I was born into a family consisting of my mother, father, and my older sister, by two years. Somewhere on the coast of Maine, where my father went to sea in search of lobster, was my first recollection, where the cold ocean breeze kept my hair in constant disarray, and the slightest taste of salt never went away. We weren't there very long, so the home we had is a memory lost in the wind. It was decided we should travel west, see the world, and embrace the chances of a new environment. We crossed the mighty Mississippi, and headed for the mountains of Colorado. It was summer, but they were still wearing a winter coat when you approached a summit. Montana and Idaho were rich in farmland, and a surprising variety of native accents, from German and Polish, to Scottish and Swedish, a true blending of nationalities, hard working one and all. Of all the things I learned about, from everyone we met, I think it was an international work habit that impressed me most of all. So, somewhere on the road to California I started thinking about what I wanted to do with myself, who was I supposed to be. The Pacific Ocean, its warm summer winds, and sandy beaches became our home, but only for a little while. Gradually it became clear to me, we were not in search of a new job, not it was a lifestyle, a continuing journey, a restless predilection for seeing, in person what was just beyond the next hill.

And thus our travels continued, headed back east, this time to North Carolina, and further south to New Orleans, which is where we found this old house. The rent was cheap enough, since it had not been occupied in several years. It was a messy place with broken windows, and creaky doors that wouldn't shut. Our first night was a living nightmare. You couldn't sleep with all the creaks and groans induced by the wind blowing through from room to room, uninhibited by walls or doors. It was a terrifying night that didn't want to end. I ran and jumped into bed with my folks, only to discover everyone was there, and no one got a wink of sleep the entire night long. Once I heard the crash of a metal bucket being hurled down the stairs, and then the sound of breaking glass, a window we assumed. Such a long and seemingly perilous night to be locked up in this house. The next day, we called up the owner, inquiring about the sights and sounds of this old house. He just laughed and welcomed us to his family tree, a bunch of harmless ghosts that refused to disappear. He advised us to introduce ourselves, and try to get along. One of them, his brother Harry, was an alcoholic, so just leave him a bottle of beer every night. He had passed away due to a car wreck. In fact, they had all died in the same accident. Well, we were out of funds for now, and had no where else to go. Another day, and another night had arrived. We gathered in the family room, anticipating being joined by our new family guests. Brother Harry was offered a cold beer, and we heard a soft ahhh. His sister Martha was offered a new old dress, and we were rewarded with a tinkering of laughter. From that moment on, we were all friends, and quickly learned to cohabit this old house. We got used to the creaks and groans, actually rather comforting. We always keep a six pack in the frig, and a fresh array of dresses can be found in the guest room, Martha's room. When I tell my new friends at school about our live in company, they just laugh, and say quit kidding around. The funny thing is that none of them has ever spent the night in our old house, where they could meet our newest family members. How about you? Are you going anything tonight?

Cloudy Days

Many a cloudy day has come my way, blown on winds of destiny. Some I remember, while others are like stories passed from one generation to the next. I remember the first time I met Santa Claus, a terrifying event in my early years, a time for tears. I remember crossing the Atlantic on this massive passenger liner, what a trip, I wouldn't miss. My first train ride was in a foreign land, from France to Germany. This was where I began my education. I remember locking myself in a bathroom, not on purpose, and having a switch laid across my backside, a lousy day, I had to pay. My first puppy dog was a pure white German toy Spitz, who would run away and find a way to get as dirty and greasy as he could. I loved him so, he had to go. I remember all the highways we traveled on, come and gone. So many restless miles, from state to state to state, from coast to coast, they just blew on by, and said goodbye. So many schools in distant places, and different faces. Newer teachers, indifferent features. As I grew older, my sense of values was challenged on many levels, different jobs, in different cities. And then there were the ladies. I fell in love while I was in the fourth grade. During a school meeting, in the auditorium, she was awarded a prize of some sort, but when they called her name, I laughed out loud. And then we met, I can't forget. Time moves on, sometimes quickly, and sometimes it seems to drag on forever. Summer vacations were the best. We went camping with our neighbors, and fishing too. My friend from next door and I always brought back a full stringer, our fathers didn't, luck was hours, hearts and flowers. High school and college were a challenge for me, ah sweet destiny. Was my future set? I can't forget, a cloudy day, I was swept away, a troubled time, I lost my mind. An accident, my time was spent trying to heal my head, but up ahead, I saw the light, and had to fight just to be alive, and find a way for me to survive. And I will, but better still, I finally found what I was supposed to be, inevitably, my date with destiny, is sharing my words and thoughts with anyone, anywhere who cares to listen and understand, I'll shake your hand. Thank you for this opportunity.

Our Time

My time, your time, our time, the time for humanity resolves irreflexively, and inconsistently for all of us until there is nothing left. You spend your time at work tensely and tired, watching and waiting for the time clock to announce your day is done. Then, the fun begins. You meet with family and friends, a dinner, a shopping spree, perhaps a movie or a Broadway show, who knows? But the hours seem to disappear at an alarming rate. Back at home, you try to rest, you try to sleep, but nothing happens. You toss and turn, hoping to avoid the inevitable, another day on the job. The night has come and disappeared in the heartbeat of time, extraordinarily quickly. Where did it go? How are you supposed to proceed when your tired body has not yet recuperated? And time goes on, like it or not. Another day magically appears. The sun is hidden behind a darkened cloud bank, and the rains begin, a testimony to the way you look at life, at least for today. Another work week, and you cannot wait for the week to end. Your forthcoming plans include a road trip, or an airplane voyage to a distant destination, some place where a different language is most common. You practice the few phrases you happen to know and wait. Finally, your departure arrives, the sun is shining, and you are off, leaving your boring life far behind. Don't think about yesterday, only concentrate on a new and brighter tomorrow. But wait, did you pack everything you need, a bathing suit, your flipflops, some sun screen which you hope you need? Yes, you mentally remember every preparation, and you are gone, as time proceeds. You're almost there, and you cannot wait for those hours of leisure to begin, but just a moment, don't be wasting time in useless hesitation. Don't you even think about how quickly your vacation will become another distant memory. Your time on the beach, or in the swimming pool, your time with new friends, is but a fading memory. What was his name? Where did they call home? Didn't you write it down somewhere, on something like your ticket to tomorrow? Well now, such would be another story to unfold before the hands of time, both yours and mine, a fleeting sense of commonality. I just can't wait, but I suppose I must. But only for a moment, I can't be wasting all the time, after all, we only have so much, and mine is almost gone.

The General

To tell you the truth, I can't remember what year it was. My mother had my sister and me all cleaned up and ready for inspection. It seems there was a parade on this day in honor of the retirement of one of our most famous generals, Omar Bradley. Once we were on station, in San Francisco, we were directed to a field of honor, where he would troop the line. The battalions were drawn up smartly, and all the dependents were gathered together in one section. Then it began. A military band played marching music, and all the men stood to attention. A solitary jeep came into sight, and slowly started towards the line. Somehow I managed to be up front, where I could see everything. As the general's jeep approached, I saluted him, with the back handed version I had seen my old man, and his companions use. Suddenly the jeep came to a halt, and the general got out, and came towards me. He calmly said, "young man, your salute is improper." He reached down, and turned my hand into a correct salute, and walked away. My mother never said a word, not until the parade was over. But when my old man approached, she could not hold back any longer. The funny thing is, I don't know who she was madder at, me or him. Her discussion, turned into a flaming rage. While my old man grinned and laughed, she whipped my tail, and I still didn't know what I did wrong.

That was so many years ago, but it seems like it was only yesterday. At such a young age, you have no idea about what you want to be, what profession you might pursue. The thing is, I always wanted to be a soldier, to wear the uniform, and to be up front for our nation, ready to fight its wars, and enforce the peace. Foolish, perhaps, but not out of the question, or an uncertainty. In high school and college, I was involved in R.O.T.C., and did very well. Growing up U had all these toy soldiers, and after reading about historical battle fields, I would recreate them, trying to find a better solution, one with lesser casualties. But, most generals are much more interested in results, not casualty lists, the means provide results. Well, not to me. Consider the comparison of Bull Run, and Omaha Beach, both with horrendous casualties, with soldiers rushing into an almost certain death. Oh my God! There had to be a better way, don't you think? So many lives thrown away, so many families torn apart. Disgraceful is the word that comes to mind. Yes, the scourge of Europe had to be stopped, and after so many years of conflict, we had to find an end. I have seen the graveyards of Normandy, and like so many visitors found a plethora of teardrops falling from my eyes, gently caressing the ground where they shed their blood, and gave their lives.

There should never be such an event ever again, and yet those lousy wars persist, from Tel Aviv, into the sands of the middle east, tyrants find a way of dominating, and defiling humanity. The lists go on and on, as do the wars to eliminate them, but they never do. There always seems to be another general, trying to take over his part of the world, trying to dominate his version of society. The world courts have no control over despots who murder and defile humanity. Is there a final answer, or are we just biding time until someone pushes the button, and our world will reach an end, blown into oblivion? God help us all.

Life and Living

Life and the act of living can be so incredibly complicated, that we find ourselves lost in space and time. Sometimes the simplistic beginnings of another day are the most elusive and difficult decisions we have to make. Is it going to rain today? Is it going to be hot or cold? What should I wear? Should I drive to work, take the bus, or just walk? Complicated? Not really, but necessary. You might catch a cold walking in the rain, or slip and fall if it snows. So maybe you should ride. I don't know, but in the end, does it really matter? Rain, snow, walk, ride. The simple things that impact us on a daily level. But, more importantly, they are just the beginnings, a prerequisite to what awaits down the road of today, leading us into tomorrow. A day of working in the sun will have you sweating, and wishing it wasn't so darn hot. On the other hand, when it's freezing outside, and you can't feel your fingers, all you can think about is last summer. I know, where am I going with this plethora of questions? Give me a second, and I'll get there, I promise. What is missing, and the most important Segway is the matter of human contact. None of us can control the weather, all we can do is talk about it and complain. Where did all that rain come from? The weather forecast called for hot and sunny days for the entire week. What are you going to do after work, especially if it keeps on raining? I think I'll catch a cab, maybe ride through the park and watch the squirrels trying to stay dry. All this rain will really make the grass grow in a hurry, and eventually make the flowers bloom. I like it like that, don't you? In the springtime and early summer, you can almost see mother nature coming to life in all her spectacular and beautiful ways. You can smell the lilac and honeysuckle, and watch the bees feeding away, and accidentally spreading the seeds of their chosen flowers. Can you imagine what would happen if this vital process was delayed, or interrupted? I can't, or don't want to, because this is what it's all about. A planted seed grows prolifically, and offers the aroma of life and the living. The many faces of mother nature can be the smallest animals, the birds and bees, or the growing grass and blooming flowers, and in the end, we all need those rainy days. The thunder and lightning, I can do without. But, if it didn't rain profusely, the Nile delta wouldn't provide for generation after generation of farmers and their lived stock. So many locals wouldn't eat or prosper, would they? The local markets would turn into sand, and blow away. When we were young, we enjoyed playing in the sand, at the beach, and swimming in the sound. But, that was yesterday, and we had the time to waste. So, what does tomorrow have to offer, a tornado, a thunderstorm, punctuated with destructive lightning bolts? Maybe, or just a soothing, gentle mist of rain to wash away the tears of yesterday, and offer us another day of life and the living.

Last Night

I am compelled to ask, where were you last night? You called to postpone our usual dinner night and said you had somewhere else to be. Knowing you like I do, I just assumed you had a dinner date. In a moment of sobriety, and a feeling of pure angst, there was nothing I could say to you that compelled another chance. I have exposed my deep emotions, and revealed a loving heart, but when you're off with someone else, it tears me all apart. I'm sitting here, I couldn't sleep, embraced by memories. I have no right to tell you how to live your life imperviously without me. There was a time, I love you so, a moment of reflection, but now I feel, so much revealed, a tragedy suggested.

You live your life in search of love, but then you hesitate. Is she the one you've waited for, the subtle hand of fate? If you take the time to question everything you see, all there is for you to see is fate or destiny. The hand of God, or father time, a dream or fantasy, you only hope to know the truth about your destiny. A travel plan, another man, a dinner date for two. An airplane trip, a sailing ship, another night with you.

With open arms I feel the pain of lovers you have lost. A tragedy for you and me, an over powering cost. It's always harder when you say it never really happened. But subtle lies will emphasize the cost of self deception. You took a chance on pure romance, another fantasy. I believe in destiny, come take a chance with me. The memories I'm living with, would tell me this is true. Still holding on, I'm not so strong, I want to be with you.

Tomorrow's just another day, a lull in space and time. Affectionately remembering those days when you were mine. I want to hold you in my arms, and whisper in your ear, you are all I'm living for, I love you so my dear.

Think I do, and Then I don't

It's amazing how a gentle breeze can turn into a raging storm. The clouds build, and thunder roars over the far horizon. A piercing flash of lightning, and all the lights are gone. The rain seems to waver on the wind, and suddenly drenches the earth, including you. Sometimes you run and try to beat the storm, and others find you laughing and splashing through puddles, without a care in the world. Sometimes you wake up with a throbbing headache, and usually you don't. Sometimes you enjoy those private moments in your car, on your way to work. But, some days you simply dread arriving at the same old place, where you will be seeing the same old crowd. And sometimes you walk through the doors, your head filled with ideas for profit, or maybe sometimes a certain someone who makes it all worthwhile, has your mind under control. Sometimes your life goes racing by like a howling wind, and all you can think about is shelter, a cozy fire, a soft set of sheets, and a relaxing story, to give you shelter, to keep you warm. In the still of the night, which sparkles and glows, the unknown leads you into the arms of another crazy day. Should I wear red or black? Should I leave a little early? Don't want to be late. And after work, should I just head on home, or meet the guys and have a few? Questions and answers, I think I do, and then I don't, I think I will, and then I won't. The uncertainty can be frustrating, or in turn uplifting and satisfying, you never know, We all look back at our moments of success or failure, offset by a chance selection, a moment of pure elation and uncertainty.

When all is said and done, the only thing that really matters is your moment in the sun, where nobody has any influence or authority over you. The only entity you must answer to is yourself! No more bias or selection, no more hidden agendas or disappointments. Every morning when you awaken, the whole world lies at your feet, so attack, enjoy, experiment. Knowing deep in your heart that nothing is impossible, and every breath you take is like the first one. So, breath my friend and the whole world will open up for you, and if you have an extra moment, mention my name, please.

Just A Man

Foolish, fearless, angry, arbitrary, sometimes ridiculous, often redundant, occasionally casual, religiously soulful, and most of all truly sorry. Words or phrases that dictate my emotions, how I feel about you, and how much I miss our lost relationship. The realization that you are gone tears at my heart and soul. After all is said and done, I am just a man trying to make the best of my existence, and who is still in love with you, and I will always be. I love the little things you do, such as making sure your makeup is simply perfect. I love how your hair embraces and defines a lovely face, and reveals a soul searching smile that illuminates everything you see. I love to listen to you rattling along about the days traumatic phone calls and accepting all those so's. And here we are, you and I, stuck on the treadmill of life, uncertain of today or tomorrow, struggling through another pause in time, not really knowing who or where we are. In such a dangerous and fluid world what is there to depend on? Who can you rely on to give you advice and reassurance that everything will be alright? Surely not your parents, they are from another generation slowly and regrettably passing away. The pressures of a modern generation seem to profoundly grow with every passing day. The simple things have become more complicated. Even when we were young the paths of tomorrow were there for us to see, to question, and change of we wanted to. But, with the roaring tide of today, you can hardly hear yourself think or elucidate about your goals, about your wishes and hopes, about your dreams. So, what is left, what makes sense, what can you really change for better or worse?

Reality says we are not meant to be alone. We shouldn't have to face such a problematic existence by ourselves. The decisions that effect our individualistic life should be our own choosing. The problem is we are rarely on our own and allow moments of emotion to control and dictate what we want out of life. It shouldn't be this difficult. What each of us is looking for and need most of all, is a partner, an acquaintance, a dear friend, and a lover. Someone who has the same values, similar dreams and emotions and is the singular entity, the missing puzzle piece that fits so well, and makes the world go around. Believe me when I say, I hear you, I know what you are talking about, because I have been there in this lonely unforgiving world, and I still am. The funny thing is, I have known all along what would make me happy, what would make my life and all it's toils and frustrations truly worthwhile, and it could only be you, it always was, and always will be.

God Help Me

God help me, I just received the news that my younger sister has been diagnosed with a incurable disease and has less than two years to live. Her tearful phone call was the last thing I ever wanted to hear. We have spent a lifetime kicking, screaming, laughing and crying over the most unimportant daily occurrences anyone could imagine. The funny thing is all the fighting and crying only brought us closed together. I don't think either of our parents were vaguely aware of the sibling animosity that permeated all those long car trips, or the voyage across the Atlantic, they had other things to attend to. My father passed a long time ago, my mother a few years ago. Every tragic moment along with certain memories, can only illustrate the undeniable closeness we felt for each other. When one of us got in trouble, the other would be waiting in the wings just to be sure the other was alright. Outside of our home, no one had better offend or attack my little sis unless they were prepared to deal with me. And that is just the way it was and still is today.

Now, I must pray for some help from someone more powerful and diligent than me. My sisters life revolves around her family, especially her grand kids. She has been financially available for her kids, and their kids, a series of debts never to be repaid. The love and time she has dedicated to their growth and maturation is irreparable. Their birthdays and every holiday provided a series of celebrations ongoing and never ending. The singular question that haunts me is what am I going to do without her? Who am I going to talk to and complain to? Whenever she has an appointment, I pick her up and drive her to her destination, it's become my job, and a reason to spend some time together. There is no one else to take her place, no one.

I have been alone for longer than I care to remember. But, she has always been there if and when I needed someone to talk to. And now what? She was always there for me, even when I almost died on my motorcycle. I woke up from my coma, and there she was. This is not a dream, I wish it was. The upcoming days and months are not enough for me. I could express my affection and devotion with every breath I take, and it wouldn't be enough. It's getting late and although I know that sleep will be more evasive than usual, I think I have to try. Maybe tonight will be spent remembering all the places we have seen. Even now I remember chasing Frosty around the trailer park, and the thunderstorm that toppled our TV antennae. I remember floating down a fishing stream, not that she enjoyed the sport. I remember boring days behind Montgomery Wards, and losing my house key, funny and not so much. All those days and years of our lives were spent together, the best times of my entire life. I'll talk to you soon sis. Love ya!

Thoughts of You

In my memories, somewhat jaded by time and circumstance, some things or events stand out and demand recognition. I have a sister who means so much to me, I don't know the words to fully explain her significance. We are almost two years apart, which would explain my indifference at her birth. Just another day when my mother was somewhere else. I don't even know if our father was present, I never thought to inquire. He was a soldier and might have been on assignment at either birthday. Every human being has a personal commitment or bonding with his or her mother. Growing up constantly on the move to a different state, a different town, where you were always a stranger made everyday activities more personal, more sheltered. Our mother was an R.N. and worked constantly to provide what my old man couldn't. Although she really couldn't cook at all, and we were stuck with the same menu on a never changing schedule, she tried and along the way, I learned how to cook. Over the years we became closer than most siblings, I knew what she was doing, and she knew the same about me. There were no secrets, no hidden agendas. If something, or someone was bothering my sister it became my mission to be there for her and assist her in any way I could. I never really thought about it in these terms until a few years ago, when I had a motorcycle accident, which left me comatose for a while. A lot of folks have asked me if or what I remembered and all I can say is nothing, no voices, no sounds, no feelings, I was out and almost down for the count and then I woke up. Still fuzzy on what had happened, anxious to get out of the hospital and on with my life, it took some time to realize how everything had changed. My business was gone, I could no longer climb ladders and do what had made a living for me ever again. But, there she was and still is today. I had to learn how to walk again, extremely frustrating. I lived under her care for a while and we resumed our relationship, but not for long. Being the rather stubborn individuals we are, I had to get up and out to find my way, any way to live and prosper on my own, and I have. The job I have is insignificant other than the fat it helps to pay the bills and feeds me a little better than relying on my retirement would.

My little sister has had more difficult days in recent years, she had been combating cancer in different body parts, on different levels and meanings. During two different episodes, she has survived the removal of two different tumors and seemed to have successfully survived. Then the results of her biannual visits and tests revealed something far worse, far more devastating to her and to me, pancreatic cancer. Her oncologist told her it is terminal. This devastating news had us both in tears, and angry as hell. I can't lose her. What am I going to do without her? Neither of us has given up and we won't. Modern science is always coming up with something new, a new drug or procedure. All my friends and associates are aware of what is happening, and a lot of prayers have been offered, and hopefully heard. God help me I love my sister so much and no matter what happens, I always will.

Lord Death

Lord Death approaches stealthily, not one to be expected.

Some darker days, indifferent ways on which to be reflected.

Quaint memories of days gone by, a lucid taste of time.

The history of who we were, a fading mystery rhyme.

We don't expect the hand of God to take our life away.

The angel standing next to you, I'm told is here to stay.

You live your life, good or bad and search the hallowed field.

Who you are, a fallen star, could never be concealed.

A message sent for you to hear, a whispered memory.

In time you'll find your way back home, a date with destiny.

Your loving heart still beats for me and always will my dear.

I hope you hear my prayer for you, it's meant to be sincere.

One last time I'll touch your hand, as tears fall from my eyes.

You left me here, alone my dear, it's hard to realize.

A bunch of roses, a touch of dust, a coffin in your grave,

A whispered prayer to God above, your heart is his to save.

Tomorrow's just another day, spend wishing you were here.

The love we have for you my dear, will never disappear.

The This Is

You see, and the thing is, I don't have the slightest clue about anything at all. I've been wandering around this world of ours for seventy years and haven't learned anything substantial in all that time. I thought I wanted to play baseball, but that requires a certain level of talent I never had. Oh, I tried and succeeded on a lower level, but not where I wanted to be and thought of where I should have been. Then there was golf, the most demanding game I've ever tried, and again I was competent, and competitive on a certain field of endeavor. But after all is said and done, those were only games. Moving forward, I became involved in martial arts, and eventually trained others in self defence. Now we're talking. I went up in rank and ran out of time. I had jobs to do, and a family to feed. Onward! I spent a lot of money on a bike, and quite a bit of time on the road. The thing is, there's nothing like the wind in your face, and the sound of the bike in between your knees. I traveled from coast to coast and everywhere in between. Loved it and then I wrecked it. Don't know what happened, and it really doesn't matter. When I finally woke up, everything had changed. The thing is, you can't wreck a ride and come out without some kind of injury. Just aint happenin', no sir not usually. Lost my boke and my girl. The thing is when you don't have a job and can't even walk in a regular way, things get rather complicated and confusing. What am I supposed to do now? Well, a lot of time went by and I started writing. Why? Beats me, it was something to do, and once I got started, just couldn't stop, and I haven't. So, what to write about? Hmm, maybe love, maybe mother nature, maybe about God and the universe. The thing is, I have never been successful at love. Oh, I've tries over and over again and lost. I've never really studied mother nature, although I have seen her power for destruction, and the beauty of her flowers and the gentle rain that helps them grow. Incredible, don't you think? Last but certainly not least is the subject of religion. I've been referred to as spiritual, not religious, and I can accept that terminology. In my younger years my mother took me and my sister to church, a vain attempt on her part. I believe a religious point of view cannot be taught only given by the powers that be.

The thing is, and what I have been leading up to is, a missing part of me. Not a game, or an occupation, or even a ride down a dusty road, but the most important part of my life, and that would be my beloved sibling, my cherisher younger sister, and now she's gone, passed away and left me here all alone. If God is listening, and I'm told He hears everything, then I would ask Him to take care of her, make her days most pleasant and peaceful. One more thing, please tell her how much I miss her and how much she is loved. Thank you.

One More Time

Here I go again. My little sister passed away not long ago. Every day I find myself anticipating her phone calls. We used to be in contact at least every other day. The funny thing is, I was into certain sporting events and she liked her soap operas. When she called it would be in between her shows and right in the middle of a game, and my calls always seemed to be at a critical point or story line. But no matter what we were watching, it became secondary to what we had to say to each other. She would vent on family problems and I would listen until she finished. Feel better now, a common question? Yes, the inevitable reply. I became her willing driver to her doctor visits. You see, she had been fighting various forms of cancer for many years. She never gave up, not after chemo and radiation and more than one surgical procedure. Each time she would recover and get back into her routine, until the next episode presented itself. These were days when we grew so close together. We laughed and cried, often at the same time. Anyone who met her became her friend. She had a way of making people smile. I don't know how many people miss her, I'm betting there are quite a few and of course, I do. The generations of her kids and grandkids, and great grandkids can only visit her emotionally, and they do.

Now she lays in close proximity to our mother. She chose cremation and there is a place reserved for me right beside her. Patience has never been one of my attributes and nothing really changes. I miss my sister in so many ways, every single day. I miss her laugh and see her tears. I watched her grow and disappear. With every passing day I try to prepare myself for when my time arrives, and with age comes a certain point of view, the inevitable and uncontrollable. We have lived an eventful life. We have loved and built our families. But most of all, when all is said and done, we had each other and we always will.

Mysteriously

In the midst of another mysterious and inconsequential evening, I find myself living without meaning, without any eventuality. Who am I? why am I still trying to communicate? In my lifetime I have come to know the means, the veracity of talking to my fellow man. A philosopher I'm not, a lost dreamer I will always be. And this it begins. Another reluctantly uncertain day, another devious but oblivious opportunity. A chance partaken of and frivolously tossed into the wind. Listen if you will, verify if you can, but proceed at all or any cost. The mind is a truly fragile entity, easily twisted and misunderstood, but never truly dominated. Your thoughts are your own, and inevitable results on another plain of mediocrity. All hair the future, a victim of the past, a vision of possibilities. Who we were, a yesterday. Who we are, a mystery. The past seems to meld into another day, and then proclaims the knowledge of tomorrow. The humanity of man has impacted our little universe. What compels us to proceed is the unknown. What the future holds could be dynamic, overpowering and inevitable. In the mighty throes of destiny, we are all overcome, a mere vestige of what might have been.

No one wants to pass, to be here and suddenly your gone. No one knows the timetable of destiny which permits the inevitability of man. Much as a storm cloud passing overhead, when will it consummate? What will it dominate? Such are those teardrops falling down, a dynamic repercussion of a historic event, lucid and philosophical. The message, obtuse, the meaning undeniable. In the given moment, we are all dynamic and mysterious. Humanity verses history, a dilemma not easily decided. The inevitability of man, a vision or the charade of destiny? Are we but puppets, dancing and cajouling amidst the propriety of time? Perhaps a vision, a portrayal of necessity, an undeniable prerequisite for tomorrow. Men we are, or hope to be, a symbolic and repetitive state of mind. Curiosity dominates and subscribes to the desire to be more than we are able. Humanity was born in an instant and continues to proliferate, some brilliant and some rather lacking, but each and everyone so worthwhile because in every soul, in every heartbeat lies our destiny and all are touched by the powerful and inescapable hand of God.

Printed by Libri Plureos GmbH in Hamburg,
Germany